Boundaries and Pleasant Places

The Revd Canon Enid R. Morgan was one of the large group of waiting women deacons ordained priests in the Church in Wales in 1997. At the time she was Director of Mission for the province leading a team of executive officers. A deacon since 1984, she had, while bringing up three sons been editor of *Y Llan*, the weekly Welsh newspaper of the Church and was the first editor of an ecumenical magazine called *Cristion*. A regular broadcaster, she worked for nine years in a four-church rural parish near Aberystwyth. Following ordination to the priesthood she has returned to parish ministry and is now Vicar of Llangynwyd with Maesteg, and an Honorary Canon of Llandaf Cathedral.

Boundaries and Pleasant Places

*Healing Division in
the Church and the World*

Enid R. Morgan

CANTERBURY
PRESS
Norwich

First published in 2004 by the
Canterbury Press Norwich
(a publishing imprint of
Hymns Ancient & Modern Limited,
a registered charity)
St Mary's Works, St Mary's Plain,
Norwich, Norfolk, NR3 3BH

www.scm-canterburypress.co.uk

British Library Cataloguing in Publication data

A catalogue record for this book is available
from the British Library

ISBN 1-85311-526-6

Typeset by Regent Typesetting, London
Printed and bound by
Bookmarque, Croydon, Surrey

Diolch Gerald

Contents

Rough Guide   viii

Preface   xi

Introduction   1

1 Nurse Logs: Trees and Peoples   6
2 Power and Politics: God on the Boundary   26
3 Peoples at the Hedge of Thorns   47
4 Between Men and Women   69
5 Communicating and Language   95
6 Between Public and Personal: 119
   The Lament of History
7 Past, Present and Future   144

Notes   163

Index of Subjects and Names   167

Rough Guide

Mae'n digwydd yn anorfod,
fel dwr yn dod o hyd i'w lefel,
ond bob tro yr agoraf lawlyfr teithio
'rwy'n hwylio heibio'r prifddinasoedd a'r golygfeydd,
ac yn tyrchu i strydoedd cefn diolwg y mynegai,
a chael fy mod yn Ffrainc, yn Llydäwr;
yn Seland Newydd, Maori;
yn yr Unol Daleithiau – yn dibynnu ar ba ran –
rwy'n Nafacho, yn Cajwn, neu'n ddu.

Y fi yw'r Cymro Crwydr –
yr Iddew ymhob man.
Heblaw, wrth gwrs, am Israel.
Yno, rwy'n Balestiniad.

Mae'n rhyw fath o gymhlethdod, mae'n rhaid,
fy mod yn codi'r grachen ar fy psyche fel hyn.
Mi dybiaf weithiau sut beth a fyddai
i fynd i un o'r llefydd hyn
a just mwynhau.

Ond na, wrth grwydro cyfandiroedd y llyfrau,
yr un yw'r cwestiwn ym mhorthladd pob pennod;
'Dinas neis. Nawr ble mae'r geto?'

Grahame Davies

Rough Guide

It happens inevitably
like water finding its level:
every time I open a travel book,
I sail past the capital cities, the sights,
and dive straight into the backstreets of the index
and find that in France, I'm Breton:
in New Zealand, Maori:
in the USA – depending on which part –
I'm Navajo, Cajun, or black.

I'm the wandering Welshman.
I'm Jewish everywhere.
Except, of course, in Israel.
There, I'm Palestinian.

It's some kind of complex I know,
that makes me pick this scab on my psyche.
I wonder sometimes what it would be like
to go to these places
and just enjoy.

No, as I wander the continent of the guidebooks,
whatever chapter may be my destination
the question's always the same when I arrive:
'Nice city. Now where's the ghetto?'

Grahame Davies[1]

Preface

Twenty years ago I went to St Beuno's, the Roman Catholic Retreat Centre in North East Wales. At the beginning it seemed quite a big deal for a woman brought up a Welsh Baptist. The Roman Catholic priest who was to be my guide gave me Psalm 16 to look at, and it was the sixth verse that leapt off the page, stopped me in my tracks.

> The boundary lines have fallen to me in pleasant places.
> I have a goodly heritage.
> *syrthiodd y llinynnau i mi mewn mannau dymunol,*
> *ac y mae gennyf etifeddiaeth ragorol.*

What rubbish, I protested. Or at least the first bit is rubbish. Yes, there has been a goodly heritage, or bits of good heritages. But boundaries are not, or had not been for me, either pleasant or comfortable places. They are disconcerting, even alarming. On one side of the boundary people pull you back while others pull you forward. It is a place where you are undecided, and you dither. You are attracted and repulsed, trapped between the familiar and the exotic. You may be intrigued and threatened. The walls along the boundaries may get higher and higher. If you climb over you may become an intruder and a traitor at the same time. If you try to stand on the boundary with a foot in both camps you are liable to be shot – or split in two. And in any case, do not good fences make good neighbours?

Multicultural has been for a while a politically correct concept. It is supposed to be good for very different people to get along together and to appreciate each other and enjoy their rich variety. But long-lasting enmities persist between peoples who live alongside each other. Hostility thrives on knowing what *they* are like even if such 'knowing' is rooted in ignorance and fear. When there is a history of inequality and oppression, when both sides despise and fear each other, then boundary lines are thoroughly unpleasant places and the heritage is poisoned. Tribalism explodes into war. And recently the very word *multicultural* has been re-examined. For ethnic groups, particularly Muslim groups have been subjected to much increased hostility as a result of the September 11th destruction in New York and the resultant 'war on terrorism' in Afghanistan and Iraq.

The very first boundary line I had to cross was from Welsh mother tongue to English neighbour tongue. It was taken for granted that the two-year-old Welsh speaker made the effort to speak English to the six-year-old English-speaking child. Class awareness was the second boundary. My grandfather was a miner, my parents were teachers. The poshest people around were doctors and lawyers. English was presumed posh – except in Swansea where they couldn't speak proper Welsh or English! Church was English and perceived as posh, as opposed to chapel which was *gwerinol* – for folk, like us. Apostolics and Roman Catholics were beyond the fringe, Orthodox unseen, virtually unheard of. Becoming an Anglican, eventually becoming a priest, was like cutting a way through a thorn hedge.

Such discoveries could surely be seen as a normal growing process from a safe, confined and rooted background to a breadth that is both gift and privilege. But in practice a journey crossing boundaries and sometimes coming back across them is not common. Exiles or immigrants do not necessarily change the world-view of their host community – and are frequently warned off trying to do so.

On retreat at St Beuno's I began to tussle with the words of the psalm, to think about cultural roots, about living on boundaries, about crossing into different cultures, about changing and being changed. This thinking was intensified when, still a deacon but with years of parish experience, I became secretary of the Board of Mission of the Province of the Church in Wales, and especially by attending a Conference on Gospel and Culture organized by the Council for World Mission and Evangelism in December 1996 in Salvador, Brazil and in a subsequent visit to the Anglican Mission Diocese of Pelotas in the south of Brazil and a stay with Bishop Luiz Prado.

The place of discomfiture and anxiety can become a creative and exciting place – though trying to help people realize that their way of seeing things is not the only valid angle on things can be deeply frustrating. Unless crossing boundaries is experienced, and absorbed as repentance and conversion, it does not necessarily change people. Learning another language is a kind of conversion. Christians are particularly prone to imagining that their particular version of the Christian faith and community is the only correct one. My comfort zone must be God's will! But the subversive power of the gospel constantly breaks open the earthen vessels, and the fermenting wine will split open the dry leather flasks of culture.

Lent is itself a cultural phenomenon and so potentially a channel for the Holy Spirit. We managed without it in my childhood Baptist community, where it was something that church and English people did. (Ignorance is a great preserver of boundaries.) We can use Lent as a chance to think things through, to reflect on things in the light of Scripture and emerge at Easter, changed. Hence the title *Boundaries and Pleasant Places*.

To those who love the earthen vessels and the leather flasks, and to those who are impatient with them, I hope this book will be food for thought and substance for prayer.

Llangynwyd
Easter 2004

Introduction

The early Christian Church nearly foundered on matters which most people find difficult to understand today. The issues seem in retrospect to be either arcane or trivial. Did new Christians have to obey the dietary laws of the Jews? Did they have to give up pork and shellfish? Could a Jewish Christian enter the house of a Roman? Was it right to paint portraits of Jesus? Should women cover their hair and could they speak in public? Were they 'unclean' at their menses? More painfully, did non-Jewish men have to be circumcised?

Saul of Tarsus, a Pharisee but also a Roman citizen calling himself Paul, had thought such things immensely important. His concern for these issues of cultural and religious identity was part of his early extreme hostility to the new sect which claimed that the crucified rabbi, Jesus of Nazareth, was the Messiah, and Servant/Son/Word of God. Paul made a list of the things that mattered to him before his blinding confrontation with Jesus on the Damascus road. First there was circumcision, the sign in flesh of being a Jew in covenant relationship with God; his tribe, Benjamin, being a Hebrew of the Hebrews; being a stickler for the regulations in the Law, that is, a Pharisee; all these things made him a persecutor of the new faith. After his conversion he counts all this to be so much rubbish (Phil. 3.8).

Saul/Paul – the two names that indicate his double status as Jew and Roman citizen, living on the boundary – leaps over the dividing wall between Judaism and the rest (the gentiles, the nations, the others), and is prepared to ditch all that was valuable to him in order 'to win Christ and the power of his resurrection'. He moves out of the world of Jewry into the world of the gentiles, the world of Greece and Rome. Paul, the Jewish Pharisee, changed from a commitment to the small elect nation, and became a passionate and uncompromising bearer of the new gospel to everyone. He was followed around for years by conservative Jewish Christians, perhaps old colleagues, for whom the religious culture of Judaism was an essential part of the package. Paul's view was that Judaism refused the freedom of the gospel. Many conservative Jewish Christians feared that Paul was betraying the covenant for which their forebears had fought so bitterly. Later Christians interpreted this as a rejection of Jesus and wrote up the story accordingly. It was a fracture, a rejection that points the way to the demonizing of the Jews; the long road leads via the pogroms to Zionism, the Holocaust, the tragic alienation of Palestine, the polarization of opinion within Israel. The present apparently insoluble conflict between the state of Israel and the Palestinians radiates into the hostility between radical Islam and the materialist so-called Christian West.

It is not only Judaeo-Christianity that allows the core of its experience of God to be tangled up with cultural issues. It seems to be as true of Islam as it is of Christianity. It is strange that faith in Allah, the all-merciful, does not override African cultural loyalty to the genital mutilation of little girls. It is strange that patriarchy subverts both Allah and God the Father of Jesus in infantilizing women, so that today they cannot drive cars in Saudi Arabia. Married women in Britain could not own property until the Married

Women's Property Acts of the nineteenth century. In many Islamic societies ordinary people will talk about God as did the quarrymen of North Wales and the coal miners of South Wales in the twenties and thirties of the twentieth century. Western Christians today seem much shyer of God. Curious cultural and economic forces have been at work to produce post-Christian cultures in which theology is not discussed.

Sometimes those who have lost faith cherish the culture most fiercely. Islamophobic attitudes are not the preserve of believing Christians alone. Does the gospel have anything to say on the matter? When you start to look at the Gospel narratives with this question in mind you begin to see clues that suggest that Jesus was intensely aware of the problem. He challenged many of the customs and laws of Judaism, saying 'You have heard it said by men of old, but I say to you . . .'. In the Gospels we see traces of the way in which the Christian community struggled to hold on to essentials while ditching non-essentials.

Many of the present divisions within the churches, many of the divisions between Judaism, Islam and Christianity are to do with culture and custom. In Europe gospel and culture were tightly woven together, but now seem to be unravelling. Is it possible to live purely by gospel? Often we simply lapse into another churchy culture. It is difficult to imagine a gospel untinged by cultural assumptions. In the first century Christians described themselves as 'sojourners', people who were not citizens, who didn't belong to the culture around and did not regard themselves as bound by the supremacy of the state. Is that possible today?

Jesus warns us that 'Where your treasure is, there will your heart be also.' We treasure our cultures, we need them for our human intercourse, but we can easily allow the culture to define us and so we learn to fear the 'other', that which is not ours. The arguments over immigration policy, the language of 'tidal waves' and 'swamping' in the media cloud the issue of how to exclude the criminal and how to enable new groups to acclimatize, contribute and communicate. The urge to exclude the alien from our culture and our comfort zone is seen in the argument over clergy who are homosexual. The ferocity and passion of those who judge and condemn and seek to drive out gifted and remarkable people is an alarming illustration of the way in which cultures seek to exclude. It is vividly inappropriate for the Christian Church to 'purify' without compassion or self-understanding

It is very uncomfortable; it feels like betrayal to turn our backs on things which on reflection are not the essential part of the gospel that we had thought. But W. B. Yeats wrote:

Where but in custom and in ceremony
Are Innocency and Beauty born?[1]

We keep our treasures in earthen vessels, and we can end up cherishing the earthen vessels more than their contents. Jesus was constantly endangering the earthen vessels; he himself pointed out the impossibility of putting new wine in old bottles. He was feared and hated for it.

This book will try to look at expressions of culture – mainly traditional ones – that may or may not be compatible with the gospel. It will seek to undermine our unconditional allegiance to our present comfort zone, and to heighten our awareness of the contradictions and limitations of the idea of a Christian culture. It will offer stories of cross-boundary, transcultural journeys which will enable us to enjoy our huge variety of cultures as gifts of

God, help us grow humble and wry about our certainties and treasures, and be readier to recognize our idolatries for what they are.

I

Nurse Logs: Trees and Peoples

I went to Seattle in 1997, in response to an invitation to
preach at the annual *Gymanfa Ganu* (hymn singing and
cultural festival) of the Welsh communities in North
America. It is a strange experience for a Welsh-speaker
from Wales to arrive in the *Gymanfa* and be surrounded by
Americans of a distinctly Republican temper. They appear
less passionate about their roots than the Irish Americans
do, but when they sing, they sing with an old-fashioned
fervour you rarely hear in Wales today. It is as though their
Welsh identity has passed through a filter labelled 'hymns'
which has sieved out anything else that is recognizably
Welsh. Since much of American society is still chapel- and
church-based in a way no longer known in Wales, they sing
the hymns with unashamed and sentimental gusto, only
partly understanding the words, but identifying with what
they think the hymns represent. This is ours. These hymns
are where we came from. A Welsh poet of the 1940s,
T. Rowland Hughes, writing about the still flourishing
chapels of Wales, claimed rhetorically:

> *O'r blychau hyn y daeth ennaint ein doe a'n hechdoe ni.*
> From these boxes came the balm of our yesterdays.[1]

In a sense one travels backwards in time to meet these
Welsh Americans. The real, present-day life of Wales with

its National Assembly and its secular public discourse is unknown and of little interest to them. Disconcertingly, you go to America expecting to find the future but find that you have flown backwards. An equivalent experience for the English might be a trip to the main morning service in an Anglican cathedral in India. In New Delhi you might find the 1662 *Book of Common Prayer* still in use together with *Hymns Ancient and Modern*. Anglican expatriates hang on to the familiar forms of childhood.

On our American trip we had determined that we would also visit the Olympic peninsula beyond Seattle. It lies at the very furthest north-west corner of the forty-eight United States, further west than Vancouver and Puget Sound to the north. We wanted to spend some time at the Makah nation's Indian reservation during their annual Tribal Festival in the little town at Neah Bay. Indian reservations can be notoriously depressing places for the residents and the visitor, but this was not our experience.

It was not until late in the nineteenth century that the white settlers made serious efforts to get to grips with the Makah, a tribe whose word for food is simply the word for fish. Their whale-hunting lifestyle was destroyed; they were expected to become potato-growing farmers despite the unsuitability of the terrain, with its thick forests and heavy rain. Other villages were moved to Neah Bay and children were forced into schools where they were punished for speaking their language, had their hair cut and were forced to wear American-style clothing.

The Tribal Festival had a curiously familiar atmosphere because it was rather like the Welsh National Eisteddfod as it used to be in the 1960s. We were travelling backwards again. There was the same mix of touching and tatty, the same lack of economic confidence. There were competitions not in poetry and song but in the canoe races in the bay and in team sports. More than half the 1,500-strong tribe live beyond the reservation, but hundreds return every year to enjoy gambling games, a mobile sweat lodge and stalls selling Indian fry-bread. It was all gloriously mixed up, tourist tat alternating with wonderful contemporary Native American art. The Welsh have an unofficial second national anthem *Ryn ni yma o hyd* (We're still here) which would suit the Makah Tribal Festival really well. In it they too might celebrate their survival against the odds.

The Eisteddfod atmosphere was echoed again in the dancing displays in the evening. This was not the popular and athletic pow-wow dancing, but solemn, even sacred dances performed with great concentration and dignity. The audience, the greater part made up of parents and supporters, sat on benches arranged around three sides of the high school gym. It resonated with that sense of emotional commitment, earnestness in transmitting a tradition to a new generation which permeate an Urdd youth eisteddfod at home. A woman sitting next to me proudly pointed to a young man in the dance:

'That's my grandson! The dancing has saved him!'

'Saved him?'

'He was in dreadful trouble with drugs and drinking. Like lots of our young people. The dancing gave him back himself.'

Some older women of the tribe sat in the front row. They were elders and leaders and among them were several of the handful of people who can still speak the Makah language. In their hair they wore beaded clasps, red beads on a turquoise background in Indian style, spelling out 'Jesus

Saves'. In that community there are strong Pentecostal churches, where direct access to the Holy Spirit is the basic spiritual stance, matching their previous native spirituality. The gospel in that guise means they can belong to Christ and still be Makah.

Welsh-speakers may find that the stories of the Native peoples touch a nerve. In them they find their own long story condensed into a shorter and more violent narrative. It must be very difficult for Indians to imagine that any white Europeans can possibly identify with their experience. Through Indian eyes, all white Europeans look guilty. Nevertheless, the story of children punished for speaking their own language is also the story of the Welsh. When we rashly tried to share our story Makah listeners smiled tolerantly. How many people speak Welsh? So many hundred-thousand? They have ten Makah elders left who speak their language. There is one young couple learning the language and committed to teaching it to their new baby. Oppressed groups tend to think their story is unique, convinced they have had it worse than anyone else does. It is not easy even for the sympathetic to step over the boundaries and share that experience, especially in times when enthusiastic whites want to learn about their once-despised spirituality and become what natives contemptuously call 'plastic shamans'.

It was from the Tribal Festival that we went to the forest, from a threatened people to a threatened place. It is an area of temperate rain forest where part of the primeval rain forest survives in the Olympic Peninsula National Park despite the devastation of the logging companies. On the Pacific beaches you see strewn huge trunks and root systems carried down the rivers from up-state logging activities. There are thinner secondary-growth forests in all directions, so it is a long journey to the remaining unfelled forest. When you arrive it is mysterious, huge, very green and quietening. You stand beneath the giant trees, beside great mossy hummocks covering over the remains of old stumps and watch the air plants, the epiphytes that get all the water they need from the moist air, swinging in green veils from the branches high above. Every shade of green is lit up by slanting sunlight in the occasional storm-broken gap.

To be aware of the issues of cultural fragmentation, of human destructiveness, of the distinctiveness of peoples in all their extraordinary vulnerability, while standing in the apparently untouched primeval rain forest, is to be forced to attempt a new sense of proportion. For as you stand in the rain forest, you may see a straight row of trees looking as if it must have been planted mechanically. Yet the line is entirely natural. During a storm, perhaps 400 years ago, one of the great forest giants succumbed. It must have crashed through the branches until it lay, its huge bulk making the forest floor even darker. Gradually moss grew over it and eventually a linear growth of seedlings sprouted along the mossy line of the trunk; it is much easier for seedlings to take root there than in the darkness of the forest floor. The seedlings compete with each other; some grow into saplings and the saplings into a smaller number of young trees maturing into a new generation of forest giants – all in a row. Their roots now reach around the old trunk and down into the earth. As the old tree trunk rots away, its supportive work completed, there opens up a tunnel-like gap where visitors stand diminished and awestruck, surrounded by the massive root-systems of the new trees. The information notices at the car park tell that the fallen trees are known as nurse logs.

Some of the great cultures of the world have been nurse logs for the Christian gospel. The very different manifestations of the Church in the world depend to a considerable extent on the shape and character of these nurse logs. Judaism, Greek philosophy, Roman law, Celtic religions, Eastern cults, Germanic pantheons, and collapsed Native American faiths have all been nurse logs. Many of the nurse logs have rotted away completely, but they have changed the shape of the forest. The growth and decay of cultures is not a quiet or peaceable process; they work by struggle and competition. There is loss when seedlings compete on the mossy trunks. Human cultures grow, mature, decline or are destroyed and the competition between them is ferocious. It is not a smooth process but a savage struggle, a story told until recently only by the conquerors, a story of the kings and the generals, the battles and the armies.

Our present conflicts, the precipitate changes driven by globalization and the collapse of traditional cultures under the assault of the mass media, all produce a kind of panic. This drives people back into the security of fundamentalism in different religions, while others construct New Age spiritualities to their own taste and to meet their own perceived needs. In a world where you can pick-and-mix what you believe, comic situations can arise. Bardsey Island, off the tip of the Lleyn peninsula in north west Wales, is in Welsh tradition the resting place of 20,000 saints and it was certainly a place to which Welsh Christians of the medieval period went on pilgrimage, often at the end of their lives. It may well have been a sacred place before the coming of Christianity. Returning home on the boat from Bardsey I found myself in the company of folk who had spent the week on the island. Several had been there on their own contemporary search for meaning and one of them declared roundly that she was certainly not into 'all the Christian stuff'. Others had been meditating and 'testing the vibrations' among the rocks and in the ruins of the priory, while another couple were laden with a sackful of crystals and a heavy Tibetan prayer bowl. Crossing the tide race in Bardsey Sound was nothing to the boundaries they had already crossed.

Compared with such journeys, indeed compared with some of the offerings explored in weekend colour magazines, reading a book for Lent might seem a tame undertaking. Keeping Lent, however, going into the desert with Christ for forty days, is no small enterprise if we do it open to what Scripture and the Holy Spirit can reveal to us. Lent grew and developed into our familiar pattern when mature Christians joined with new Christians on their catechumenate journey towards baptism. New Christians were normally baptized at Easter time. Their baptism would thus be linked very closely with the remembrance of the cross, the death and resurrection of Jesus. Although we tend to think of baptism first as a washing away of sin, it has also a darker association with the death of Jesus. He spoke of his death metaphorically as 'the baptism with which I shall be baptized'. Preparation for baptism of new believers coming in from other faiths or philosophies became rigorous, and was a time in which the new believers, the catechumens fasted and prayed, were taught the essentials of the faith, in confession received forgiveness and were washed clean of all their sins. In order to encourage them in the rigour of this preparation mature or well-established Christians would walk the same journey in solidarity with them. A group from their congregation, their sponsors, patrons – companions of whom our godparents are but pale imitations – fasted, prayed and repented with them, returned with them to a state of baptismal purity and reaffirmed their baptism vows with the new believers. It was this journeying together that grew into the symbolic forty days of Lent to recall our Lord's own preparation for his ministry.

As Christ prepared for his ministry, thinking and praying through the issues which would beset him regularly, by radically reassessing his own spiritual inheritance in Judaism, so we today, by setting aside our usual pre-occupations and busyness, may make a new beginning and seek to separate gospel essentials not only from ecclesiastical and cultural clutter but from secular expectations as well.

That should help put going without chocolate or alcohol (and reading a Lent book) into perspective! The link with baptism, with dying to sin and beginning again in new life and a heartfelt preparation for that new beginning, should reinvigorate and refresh our hearts as we come around to it each year.

We cannot live without cultural patterns. We have to be rooted to grow; cultural patterns can convey gospel. But gospel is also a flowing well of living water, fresh and capable of transforming cultural patterns and turning traditional understandings upside down and inside out. Culture is water tamed, piped, put in a tank, and made useful, domesticated. Stored water, however, can become tainted; as the prophet Jeremiah observed, we can choose cracked cisterns rather than the living water of God.

This book is a reflection on the boundaries set up by culture, presuppositions, prejudices, historically formed assumptions, education, money, class, taste, family, church. What might it be like to do without these things, to pass over boundaries and still be a disciple of Christ? We might hope to value our culture and know it for what it is, to love it and sit lightly to it, to be grateful rather than proud. We might hope to discover afresh the surging, dangerous, re-creative power of the gospel, taking us into the future, creating new but temporary cultures through which we can pass to him who is Alpha and Omega.

*   *   *

The Christian faith grew out of Judaism and Judaism itself is indebted to other cultures which we glimpse in the Genesis myths and narratives of the patriarchs. The infancy of Christ narratives in Luke's and Matthew's Gospels describe a bridge from the world of Judaism over a chasm into the world of the nations. From Paul's letters we know that there were Jewish Christians who followed him around, accusing him of betraying his heritage because he suggested that the gentiles could come to God without being obedient in all respects to the Torah, to the Law of Moses. The issue of circumcision was the most critical. The book of Acts describes rather sparingly the great crisis in which the early Church discussed the issue at the Council of Jerusalem and determined how to move forward. In Acts 15.22–29 the apostles send a letter to the burgeoning gentile church, a letter with minimum requirements:

> You are to abstain from food sacrificed to idols, from blood, from the meat of strangled animals and from sexual immorality. You will do well to avoid these things.

There is no mention of circumcision, which had precipitated the crisis. It is therefore rather strange that, before the end of chapter 15, Timothy was circumcised in order not to offend the Jews who knew that his father was a Greek. It seems clear that there was a prolonged period of struggle, not satisfactorily resolved by the Council of Acts, during which the requirements made of gentile believers varied from area to area.

As far as food sacrificed to animals was concerned, the new Christians were living in a Roman culture where the meat trade was closely linked with the sacrifice of animals in pagan temples. Paul would argue that since the Roman gods had no reality it did not matter what the people who sacrificed animals to them thought they were doing. It was nothing, so it was only those with a weak conscience who would be bothered. The provenance of the steak really did not matter, but to avoid giving offence to the weak, Christians could avoid temple meat if possible. Eventually of course the problem evaporated with the demise of the pagan temples.

There is no mention in the directive from Jerusalem of the other Jewish food taboos. Human beings have strange food customs, and normally we eat what is good, pleasant-tasting, and above all, customary. The idea of eating horse meat is disliked in Britain, though more people have done so than realize it. Eating dog meat is even more taboo. Only in such instinctive revulsion have we any idea of the power of the food taboos. The minutely detailed Jewish dietary rules were to be obeyed simply because God had said so. Whatever the original cultural reason for avoiding particular foods, the religious tradition interpreted it as God's command, as part of belonging to the community of faith, the people of Yahweh. It was not and is not possible to be a believing Jew and an eater of shellfish or pork. This is both a cultural given and a religious requirement. Hence the story of Peter's overcoming of the dietary laws is a drama of considerable significance and a major part of the background to the Council in Acts 15.

In that light the moderation of the request in the letter in Acts 15 is quite extraordinary. Its most remarkable feature is the good news that circumcision was not to be compulsory for the gentiles. The widespread custom of male circumcision, often a puberty rite in African cultures, is in Judaism a sign of the covenant between God and Abraham, an act performed on eight-day-old babies which incorporates the child into a covenant relationship with God as a member of his people. Christians are aware of that as historical fact, but are not very good at imagining the power of that sign, how it had been fought for, what it meant for Jewish identity and how difficult it must have been for early Christian Jews to accept that it did not matter for gentile believers in Jesus. Today even non-believing Jews with no religious reason for retaining the custom find it very difficult to abandon the practice, for it is a sign not just of religious covenant but of ethnic identity.

Matthew's Gospel seems to have been written for Jews who were living in the wake of the Council of Jerusalem's decision. Presumably among themselves they stuck to their own usual diet and circumcised their own male babies. But if circumcision was not essential, then what was the status of their own cultural and religious heritage? It is in Matthew's Gospel that the issue is most important. Indeed it is a Gospel in which the value of the Jewish heritage is most strongly affirmed, but also in which the Jews are vigorously criticized. Matthew seems to be writing out of the agony produced in that community by the need to move on and by having to rethink their previous cultural and religious assumptions. Their struggle is on the boundary between Judaism and Christianity, between the cultural norms of their ethnic traditions of their old faith and the undesired and threatening freedom of the new faith.

Bible Study

Matthew 6.1–6, 16–21

Jesus said to the disciples:

'Beware of practising your piety before others in order to be seen by them; for then you have no reward from your Father in heaven.

'So whenever you give alms, do not sound a trumpet before you, as the hypocrites do in the synagogues and in the streets, so that they may be praised by others. Truly I tell you, they have received their reward.

'But when you give alms, do not let your left hand know what your right hand is doing, so that your alms may be done in secret; and your Father who sees in secret will reward you.

'And whenever you pray, do not be like the hypocrites; for they love to stand and pray in the synagogues and at the street corners, so that they may be seen by others. Truly I tell you, they have received their reward.

'But whenever you pray, go into your room and shut the door and pray to your Father who is in secret; and your Father who sees in secret will reward you.

'And whenever you fast, do not look dismal, like the hypocrites, for they disfigure their faces so as to show others that they are fasting. Truly I tell you, they have received their reward.

'But when you fast, put oil on your head and wash your face, so that your fasting may be seen not by others but

by your Father who is in secret; and your Father who
sees in secret will reward you.

'Do not store up for yourselves treasures on earth, where
moth and rust consume and where thieves break in and
steal; but store up for yourselves treasures in heaven,
where neither moth nor rust consumes and where thieves
do not break in and steal. For where your treasure is,
there your heart will be also.'

On Ash Wednesday Christian congregations mark the
beginning of Lent. Can we still see any life-giving significance in this piece of ecclesiastical culture? Many will have
their foreheads smudged with ash, a minimalist relic of
the old Jewish custom of pouring ash on the head as a
prophetic action of repentance and mourning. They will,
however, hear a gospel in which Jesus tells us not to make a
show of our piety but to keep our gestures, our repentance,
our religious activities discreet and private. Jesus was
brought up in a culture in which outwardly and obviously
religious behaviour earned approval. Praying, fasting and
giving alms are basic features of all the great religious
traditions; C. S. Lewis groups them with temperance,
honesty and sobriety, and calls them 'the monotonous pro-
cession of great virtues'. Jesus' critique of his own society
constantly points to the danger of fake piety, the hypo-
critical display of outward religious behaviour, while the
actual relationship with God is hollow. Motive is at the
heart of this. If it matters to you what people think of you,
if you want status in your tribe, then you will conform to
what matters to your tribe. What God demands is far more
important than what your contemporaries expect. For the
Jews, piety displayed in prayer, signs of fasting and osten-
tatious giving of alms, all earned admiration. Jesus says

such people have their due reward in the admiration of others. They should not seek any more. But if their motive is to please God, to grow closer to God, to grow in holiness of heart which God alone knows, then public display should be avoided.

There is little danger of that in Britain today. Nobody outside the Church and precious few inside are impressed by obvious piety. Within the culture of the Church we conform to expectations, certainly, but pretending to be pious is not what we need to worry about. Our culture is in this respect very different from the society in which Jesus lived. Ours is a vigorously secular society in which a religious commitment is often suspect. Churchgoing teenagers in state schools may well be baited by their contemporaries. School weekend activities take no account of church-going. Openly religious behaviour is not admired; it is thought old-fashioned, irrational, moralistic. In Judaism wearing florid religious dress, giving ostentatiously, wearing of sackcloth and ashes, the tearing of clothing in grief, all indicated a commitment to faith and to prayer – and that commitment was admired. Admiration invites hypocrisy. Hypocrisy flourishes in a society where piety and religiosity are prized and where an elite enforce standards which are to be emulated. The original religious motive slides into cultural imitation.

In Jesus' culture it was thought good to be religious. It was part of the understanding of what is good, what is just, what God commands, what is truly human and humane behaviour and what whould be rewarded in society.

One thing God has spoken, two things have I heard: that you, O God are strong, and that you O Lord are loving. Surely you will reward each person according to what he has done. (Ps. 62.22 NIV)

Reward is the issue at stake. The reward, the wage for an action is material to the discussion. The publicly pious have their reward-wage of admiration. So Jesus neatly puts his axe to the root of publicly approved goodness.

How then, according to Jesus as recorded by Matthew, are people to aspire to virtue? Matthew suggests, embarrassingly, that it depends what you want out of it, what kind of return you want for your investment of time and money and trouble. If what you want is admiration by people in your society, then that is what you get. That's it. It has no other significance. You have your reward. This word 'reward', often used by Matthew, signifies at one level 'wages', what you get in return for doing your work. You have given money in order to be admired, so be content with admiration. Matthew goes on to suggest that if you give because you love God and your neighbour, then your reward will be 'great in heaven'. If you do it in order to get that reward, you may be deeply offended when you realize that God's generous love is poured out unstintingly on the undeserving as well as the deserving. If we are looking for wages as our reward then, like the workers in the vineyard, we will be angry when the latecomers get to enjoy the very same reward as we have. God's grace is in a different category from wages or reward. God's sheer overwhelming generosity has nothing whatever to do with our deserts; it is given from love, not because of any accumulated points of virtue.

In Britain we are not in danger of being religious exhibitionists. In our church culture our danger is of not taking holiness seriously enough. When Jesus talks to his disciples about basic religious practices like praying, fasting and giving, temperate Anglicans remain curiously detached. It is as if we think we don't have to do these things properly because Jesus criticized ostentation. But if we want to live life in the light of God it is clear that prayer, fasting and giving are basic practices and we need to be committed to them, not for the good they may do us or other people, but because they form the structure around which our love of God can grow. Doing good in order to be admired or refusing to do it because only God would know, amount to the same thing.

For those who do not believe in God, prayer is not merely meaningless but can seem actually threatening. Because it is not understood it is both mocked and feared. At its most frivolous it is asking for unfair advantage, as when a tennis player crosses himself, or football fans urged to pray for the healing of a player's foot. It is justifiably mocked. When it is reported that presidential meetings in the United States begin with prayer, English papers are uneasy and interpret it as a sinister and collective abandonment of rationality, or an attempt to acquire a divine stamp of approval on questionable government policy. If they have prayed beforehand, then they must think that what they do is God's will, which must rule out any disagreement or normal political debate. When other Christians profoundly disagree with US government policy it may tend to confirm unbelievers in their conviction that prayer is a worthless activity.

It is interesting that the suspicions of the non-believers live side by side with a rather more pragmatic approach to other mind-bending or mood-affecting exercises. A burgeoning service industry of therapies is widespread and fashionable. For it is curious, even comic, how in a society that is so indifferent and even hostile to Christianity, the practice of various spiritualities flourishes. Alongside the piles of self-help, self-heal, self-consciousness books, there is a variety of therapies, from aromatherapy and crystal-poising to circle-dancing, mud packs and colonic irrigation.

The criterion for acceptability is the feel-good factor. Meditation can be shown as physically and psychologically good for you, calming and stress-releasing just as long as it has no belief factor to clutter it up. It is useful if it helps you de-stress and de-tox, if it takes its place in a battery of stratagems for coping with the urgencies of modern life. Any tinge of Christian practice, however, is rejected; prayer wheels, prayer flags, prayer bowls, prayer beads are acceptable, but not rosaries. Mantras are cool, but these contemporary, media-fed aspirations to the spiritual sit uncomfortably with the formality of liturgical prayer, and are totally extinguished by the sheer garrulousness of free prayer.

On the other hand, the popularity of retreats and multiplication of books on prayer suggest that within the community of faith prayer is nurtured. But prayer for Christians is not just a therapy, though it is certainly healing. Its healing power has to do with the relationship with God which is nourished by it. We do it not because it feels good – it often doesn't feel at all good or even interesting – but because it is where we start putting ourselves to rights, in touch with what the psalmist calls the 'well of life', and in a position to learn something small about truth, truth about ourselves, and others and God. By nurturing our relationship with that deepest reality we put our relationships with others in a clearer light. The Eucharistic Prayer says that 'it is our duty and our joy', to give thanks to God. Duty is not a fashionable concept either in regard to God or our neighbours. But in Lent, embracing what is actually our duty may well be the surest way to joy. So obeying the command of Jesus is a good place to start, or start again.

Jesus also said 'When you fast . . .'. There was no 'if' in the sentence. Christian culture in Britain does not take fasting for granted and most of us do not do it. The old tradition of fasting on Wednesdays and Fridays is largely confined to religious communities; eating fish on Fridays is long forgotten. Our society has become obsessed with food. Cooking has become an entertainment. Eating out has become far more common, while home cooking is a shrinking skill as families in which both parents work outside the home eat more and more pre-prepared food. Junk food and cheap food lead to growing obesity problems and hence a preoccupation with diets. More and more people have to control their eating for the sake of their health and for the sake of their appearance. Self-interest and vanity, in other words, are perfectly acceptable reasons for eating less. But to fast for love of God is thought pointless, and not only by non-believers.

Yet Jesus talks about prayer and fasting together. Fasting without prayer is obviously nothing to do with God, but controlling greed and gluttony is a spiritual matter. Obese Christians, addicted Christians clearly have problems, so prayer must surely be part of their struggle. Fasting, however, is not only for fatties. One of the immediate effects of fasting or dieting, at whatever level they are attempted, is to make us realize our weakness. Our creatureliness means that we have to eat and drink regularly. To limit that in any way at once makes us realize how hard it is to break a habit, how hard it is to say 'no' to immediate gratification, how easy it is simply not to bother. Perhaps that is why we try to reinforce an attempt at this kind of self-control or restraint by saying that fasting would be physically beneficial, or even financially beneficial, so that what we save on a meal might be given to some good cause. Some will eat more simply, in order to identify with the poor, and fasting or hunger-strike can all be vivid acts of protest. But, says Jesus, it is the secret fast with prayer that brings us close to God. Whether we give up meat or wine, dairy products or caffeine does not in itself matter to God at all. What matters is its effect on us and the way it can help to turn us to God, to take our bodies seriously and to accept the traditional knowledge of the value of bringing prayer and fasting together. Ash Wednesday is a good time to challenge the insipidity of our religious culture and a counter challenge to the easy gratification of our supermarket society.

From dieting to almsgiving. The very phrase 'almsgiving' has an old-fashioned ring to it, but Jesus says 'When you give . . .'. He does not question the duty to give, but he demands that it should be unselfconscious, spontaneous, loving and above all secret, anonymous. This is totally at odds with our practices in charitable giving, fund-raising and sponsoring, for these all rely on public image, even advertising. Giving alms to the needy, perceived as a duty before God who gave us all, needs to be done purely for love of God or it is sullied by other motives. For the sake of promoting a culture of giving, it might indeed be good to fund-raise, to show your little group with its giant-sized cheque presenting its gift to a charity chairman. But before God, to protect yourself from the taint of seeking public approval and even self-satisfaction and self-congratulation, then give in secret.

On this basis, Lent needs to be the time when Christians get out their household accounts, think about what they give, think about what they need, and then give. Paul suggests that the real motive for giving is gratitude. So when we consider these traditional Jewish acts of righteousness, praying, fasting and giving, searching our motives in humility is essential. It cannot be in order to win God's approval, but out of longing to know and love God more simply and unconditionally.

Questions

1 Do you recognize what ethnic/cultural/religious groups make you hostile and uneasy? What kind of ethnic jokes make you laugh? Do you know why? What do you actually know about these people?

2 Do you have a relationship with individuals from a different cultural group or race?

3 Find out how to get to know someone from a local ethnic minority. Pray for them.

4 What Christian groups make you wrinkle your nose? Pray for them.

5 When and how are you going to fast?

6 Do you have a serious Lent Box for money? Review your giving and increase it.

7 How much do you want to know God?

8 What will be your secret Lenten discipline? What reward do you get?

9 Jesus said, 'Where your treasure is, there will your heart be also.' What is your treasure?

2

Power and Politics:
God on the Boundary

Gwynllyw Farfog – Gwynllyw the Bearded or perhaps Gwynllyw the Warrior was a Welsh chieftain – what today we would call a warlord, though he might have preferred the title of king – in the late fifth and early sixth centuries. In the chaos which followed the withdrawal of the Romans from Britain he controlled an area which is best known as East Glamorgan and West Monmouthshire; it was named Gwynllwg after him. He respected neither law nor custom and when he saw something he wanted, he took it. Like other tribal leaders around him he used his fighting power to control the boundaries of his territory, and his cunning to get what he wanted from beyond his territory.

Like the farmer he wanted a wife, and knew that Gwladys, the eldest daughter of one of his most respected neighbours, was particularly beautiful. He made approaches to her father Brychan, whose territory was named after him, Brycheiniog (Brecon). Brychan was not impressed by the prospect of a son-in-law eyeing up his land as well as his daughter, so he refused permission for the marriage. Gwynllyw was a violent man, a pagan and clearly unsuitable for marriage to his Christian daughter. Thereupon Gwynllyw got together a sizeable war-band, made a raid on Brycheiniog and abducted the beautiful Gwladys. The enraged Brychan, who we must note was a Christian, led his war-band in pursuit and, so the story says, it was only the intervention of King Arthur that prevented serious bloodshed, and the couple were married.

Now Brychan had been married three times and had so many children that the total varies in different accounts. The most consistent number, though probably too neat to be true, is that he had twenty-four sons and twenty-four daughters – and all of them, so the story tells, came to be recognized as saints. Instead of being too worried about particularity of facts and numbers, we may note that this was a time of major commitment to Christianity in Wales, a commitment that affected society and its governance. Certainly Gwladys would have needed to be a saint to cope with Gwynllyw. When their first son was born Gwynllyw went off on a great celebratory cattle raid into Gwent with his war-band, and came home with assorted livestock, some of which belonged to a Christian commune ruled by one Tathyw of Caerwent – like Brychan another immigrant Irishman. Tathyw, brave soul, arrived at Gwynllyw's head-quarters to demand his property back. Tathyw had no bunch of warriors, or royal court to back him up, but Gwladys, saint as she was, seems to have persuaded Tathyw to be content with receiving back his two cows in exchange for a gesture of goodwill. He agreed to baptize the new baby, Gwladys's and Gwynllyw's first son, naming him Cadog. So the child was initiated into the Christian faith of his mother and maternal grandfather; like his mother, he would eventually be recognized as a saint, and indeed all Gwladys's other children, so the story tells, became saints, like their uncles and aunts. Since their names are given to holy sites it seems that the word saint, in the Welsh context, describes men and women who by witnessing to their Christian faith formed around themselves communities of faith.

Gwynllyw (still a pagan later in life) had a dream in which the Christian God appeared to him and promised him that he would find a valuable white ox with a black spot on its forehead on a hill overlooking the estuary of the Usk. He was after all a cattle raider – what else would he have dreamed of? The following day, Gwynllyw found that God's promise was indeed true. He was so overcome that he allowed his son, Cadog, to convert him to Christianity. Gwladys does not get the credit for this, though her forbearance must, surely, have prepared the way for Gwynllyw's eventual capitulation to Christ. Presumably her wise conduct would have laid the foundations for this conversion, for even gang leaders, warlords and kings have been influenced by their womenfolk.

So it was that the cattle raiding war-lord became a Christian and his subsequent career demonstrated the difficulty of staying chief and being true to the new and deeply subversive values of the new faith. There would be no more killing or bullying, no more abducting women or stealing other people's property. The changed Gwynllyw tried to rule his people by the new principles. This made a huge impression on his subjects and their descendants. A king who had stopped stealing – surely such a thing must be a contradiction in terms! Eventually finding the conflicting demands of faith and gang leadership too difficult, Gwynllyw and Gwladys retired to live a monastic life, and in her subsequent widowhood Gwladys became a hermit. The story claims that they took cold baths in the Usk all the year round and lived apart from each other in chastity, which is reminiscent of earlier Spartan traditions of Celtic saints who thought standing in cold water controlled the lusts of the flesh. Gwynllyw built a church dedicated to St Mary on the hill near the Usk where he found the white ox with the black spot on its forehead. That site on Stow Hill in Newport, in the diocese of Monmouth, is the site of today's cathedral of St Woollo, its name a rather ugly corruption of the original name of Gwynllyw. He was buried there after his death on 29 March, AD 523 and became revered as a saint. From cattle thief and warlord to patron saint.

This engaging if unlikely tale was composed to a stylized pattern many centuries after the life of Gwynllyw himself. The prototype for the lives of the saints was the life of St Martin of Tours, who gave up his successful career as a Roman soldier to become a monk. So the sceptical historian can dismiss such stories of the Welsh saints as inventions devised for purposes of ecclesiastical politics. There is justification for such scepticism, since many lives were written to promote the status and prestige of particular saints and their shrines. Nevertheless, Gwynllyw's life-story reminds us of the ever-present difficulties which Christian leaders have experienced when trying to live according to the faith and yet ruling according to the realities of power and politics. Such leaders lived in human societies to which they were bound, and they inherited the same epic, warrior violence and honour codes. They lived on the boundary between worldly responsibility and the demands of a faith, which called them to live according to very different standards – according to the will of God, pointing to the kingdom of God. Even as leaders they were still, in St Paul's words, sojourners in a foreign land, yet they had to live and work among people whose traditional allegiance was to power, status, riches, land and who were used to the enforcing of obedience on territorial boundaries.

Even earlier in the history of the Church than the time of Gwynllyw, people were suspicious of the new and rapidly growing faith. Christians were persecuted for not believing

in the gods of the state. Today politicians who are
Christians in Britain are constrained into being discreet
about their Christian faith. The susceptibilities of unbelievers make them very sensitive to the suggestion that
there might be a greater truth then mere self-interest. The
claim to faith makes politicians open to sharper and
sardonic scrutiny of any moral shortfalls or hypocrisy. In
the early centuries, because of a the language of the
Eucharist, Christians were accused of cannibalism which
seems a particularly nasty piece of spin by their enemies.
Second-century Christians made various efforts to explain
what the faith was about. One such effort was made in the
form of a letter to one Diognetus, an enquiring pagan who
wanted to know why the Christians made such fearless
martyrs, why they would not recognize heathen gods or
keep the observances of the Jews, why they loved each
other so much, and why God had left it so late before
revealing this truth – if it was the truth. The anonymous
author notes that you can't spot Christians as separate
communities. They don't look different, they don't eat or
dress or live in the community in any obvious way different
from other citizens, but their idea of citizenship is strange.

> They live in their motherland, but they live as pilgrims.
> They share everything as citizens; they suffer everything
> as sojourners (foreigners/asylum seekers). A foreign land
> is their mother country . . . They live on earth, but their
> citizenship is in heaven. They obey the laws, but in their
> own lives they surpass the laws. They love all, but are
> persecuted by all . . . In a word, what the soul is to the
> body, that is what Christians are to the world . . . The
> soul dwells in the body, and yet it is not of the body; so
> Christians dwell in the world and yet they are not of the
> world . . . Yet it is they who hold the world together.[1]

Jesus said simply that those who believe in him are the salt of the earth, light in a lamp, yeast in the dough. How can we nurture that kind of citizenship in our day in the face of media sneering and public dislike of all religion?

Many of the Celtic saints, though of chiefly or kingly descent, simply renounced worldly power. This was particularly true of many of the children of Brychan. The stories told of many of Gwladys's brothers and sisters suggest that the new faith called them to abandon courts and kings. This may demonstrate the influence of the desert spirituality of the fourth-century monks of Egypt. It may have been simply the result of the situation they were in, for the same difficulty emerges when Christians are a minority seeking to live according to the truth of the gospel. The difficulty is a real one today. When Christianity became a state religion in the time of Constantine, it seems that the Church became bloated with new semi-converts, and convenience believers, looking to the main chance, seeing the badge of faith as a helping hand up the ladder of power. Some of the most devout departed in disgust at this deterioration in order to keep a stricter, narrower rule of faith far from cities and towns, and as far away from other people as they could get. In Britain, when the governing Romans departed, the land fell apart politically under different warlords fighting for their own patches of ground. The same pattern can be seen in what we call today the 'failed states' of the world – Somalia, Afghanistan and Congo. It has happened particularly in many former European colonies where the problems of the past have been reinforced and allowed to fester. Whether in the Balkans or Africa or India or Iraq, an army-enforced peace cannot in the long term solve the problems of diverse peoples led by power-hungry leaders. Satan, said Jesus, cannot cast out Satan.

What makes the beginning of what historians used to call the Dark Ages so intriguing is that in Britain and Ireland it was also the age of the Celtic saints. It is the lack of documentary evidence that makes these ages 'dark'; it is doubtful whether they were any darker than later centuries of political and military turmoil. How did the new Christians and missionaries work, how did their faith and revolutionary witness transform the old paganism and tame it, how did they win admiration? The stylized semi-mythical stories of the saints written down years later have curious details that suggest some basis in fact. Historians tell us that we can't treat the narratives as 'that's what happened', but the memory of the community may retain the meaning of an experience even when facts are fragmented.

As already acknowledged above, the later Christian narrators had their own agenda of ecclesiastical influence, they wanted to produce evidence of the story of the faith, of the saints and heroes and heroines of the local church that they could present to conquering Normans, intent on imposing a different structure on Christians of the far west with their uncouth and apparently ill-disciplined ways. The Normans were bringing with them not only their genius for ruthless organization but also the whole apparatus of Gregorian reforms. In other words, travelling on the coat tails of empire and armies was extending Christian practices; local tradition was to a considerable extent to be swept aside. What a familiar story!

For example, across Ireland stand many ruined 'castles' built by English conquerors over several centuries. Shra Castle is one such fortified manor house of the Elizabethan period. Just enough remains of the building to show above the ruined doorway the motto of the Herbert family who built the place which proclaims, 'By God of might I hold my right'! Those who commissioned the carving were

Christians, but the sentiment in the mottoes is that of Ozymandias, that king of kings who commanded: 'Look on my works, ye mighty, and despair.' Shelley's sonnet sums it all up:

> Nothing beside remains. Round the decay
> Of that colossal wreck, boundless and bare,
> The lone and level sands stretch far away.[2]

Christian Europe is littered with such ruins, evidence of vain attempts to subdue and control by force of arms. Avignon and Montségur, cathedrals and dungeons point to a culture of domination and oppression. It is the mark of Cain, the murderous instinct that drives the culture of tribe against tribe, the need for sacrifice to the gods, the guilt and fear of the divine. Human beings are always ready to resort to violence and in our media-dominated age the evidence is all too abundant. Without cultural or religious sanctions to maintain a level of reasonable behaviour as a basis for law and order, the issue of keeping the peace between rival gangs and even between feral children becomes a practical matter. In the aftermath of the war on Iraq waged in spite of international law, there was a break down of law and order within the country and looting turned to self-destruction. Baghdad, as one correspondent put it, was 'a city sacking itself'. Yet there was a real psychological difficulty when the 'Christian' conquerors or liberators (choose your word according to your belief) attempted to persuade Islamic religious leaders to call their people back to honesty and good Muslim standards of behaviour. In the secular mind-set of the western media the titles used by religious leaders become terms of abuse – missionary, mullah, ayatollah. Vicar and bishop wait their turn.

Once again we may revert to the state of Britain in the

period following the withdrawal of the Romans. The Romans had maintained law and order on the fringes of the empire in part by their customary strong military rule. One subtler method of reconciling native populations to their rule was to adopt local deities if they seemed compatible; thus the Celtic gods were declared to be local manifestations of the their own gods. However, once their own power was challenged at home they had to withdraw from Britain. Organization, civil control, literacy – the manifestations of civilization – all shrank away. It was not a sudden collapse, rather a slow whittling away of the old standards while the old violence resurfaced and gained the upper hand. It is in this desperate period, when local kinglets fought each other even as the Irish, Picts and Saxons launched their deadly raids, that the myth of Arthur the Christian king has its roots. The stories of the Christians who lived then, being yeast in the dough, being salt and light to their society, come down to us through inadequate records, filtered through memory and prejudice and fear, decorated with romantic prettiness, and moulded by the political constraints of a much later time.

Why should these obscure and unreliable stories speak to us at all today? Whatever sources that were available clearly seemed useful to those local church leaders who, following the Norman Conquest, sought to argue the case for their own tribal and ecclesiastical dignity and autonomy. In our own day the early Christianity of the Celtic lands (which was in fact not a uniform phenomenon) has been laid open to a thorough reconstruction at the hands of those who perceive in it elements that appeal to them. To generalize brutally, what often emerges is a peculiar potpourri of conjecture, fantasy and wishful thinking. What we know of this period and those places is so scrappy that interpretation relies on what the interpreters want to find.

The period which is also the period of the Celtic saints has become a happy hunting ground for those disaffected from the mainstream churches of Europe. There is a search for something softer, closer to nature, less hierarchical, more – whatever you fancy! On the Internet there is even a kind of Restoration Celtic, which is a realm of the imagination. The very concept of 'Celtic' is often a holdall term convenient for outsiders, who cannot be doing with the gritty, resentful, truculent and sometimes shabby worlds of the Scots, the Irish, the Welsh and the Bretons.

The Celts, so called, shrug and go along with it, cashing in where possible. The Welsh, Irish, Scots, Cornish, Bretons today struggle with a world of European Community grants and Option 1 funding, of new parliaments and wilting tiger economies, of threats to their countryside, of prosperous immigrants they dub white settlers and of declining rural communities. Just so in the disintegration of society in the sixth century, real people had to come to terms with getting a living, enough food to eat, a bit of dignity, a something left over, an overall meaning and hope in which to make sense of their experience. For Gwynllyw a breakthrough came with the dream of a white ox with a black spot on its forehead.

There are difficult questions about power for Christians in every generation, whether they happen to live in the time of a conquering empire or within a struggling and oppressed minority. If Christians are part of the governing secular power, what is their role within the culture of domination? The Roman empire swallowed up religions and used them for service to the state. It found both Judaism and Christianity highly indigestible. So when Constantine made Christianity the religion of the empire there was an extraordinary reversal of poles, a turning inside out of what had been. Constantine himself refused baptism until near death, which is no sort of answer. But what were rulers who became Christian to do? How can they reign if they forgo the ways of power, which so often involve cruelty and theft? The Christian command to share and care for the poor whether feckless or not, is not compatible with the firm smack of government by kings and queens. If you are not to kill how can you have a warrior band – let alone an army? If you don't have a warrior band how can you defend your people against other cattle raiders? Or does Christianity become so scandalously paradoxical in rulers that they ought to take to the desert, now, as some did in the sixth century?

This is not only a matter of tension between Christians and the state. Within the Church itself there are contradictions and tensions. The Synod of Whitby in 664 was one such inner clash between the power of a reforming and successful system centred in Rome, and an untidy, recalcitrant and culturally threatened set of fringe churches in the Celtic lands. They needed reform and to be linked again with the rest of the Church, but they naturally resented and feared the ruthlessness with which it was imposed – sometimes in matters that could have borne variety. Abbess Hilda, presiding over that meeting, bowed to the greater power for the sake of peace, even though her own heart may have preferred the simplicity of the church in which she had been nurtured. That church of Cuthbert, a church of ferocious asceticism, gave way to the church of Wilfrid, a rich church of developing aesthetics and fine architecture allied to secular power.

So it has been through the history of the Church in Europe. The story of Christianity is tangled in the issue of its relationship with secular power, each side using the other for its own purposes. The struggle for disestablishment of the Church of England in Wales at the end of the nineteenth century was typical. A Church alienated from the people by its ties to social and political power was attacked by native leaders driven at least partly by jealousy and desire for political influence. It was, remarked one sharp-tongued satirist, 'a struggle between sinners and hypocrites'.

The eighteenth-century castration of the Anglican Church when bishops were appointed on condition that they voted with the Government in the House of Lords did even greater harm in Wales than in England. Whereas the Welsh bishops of the Reformation period had identified with Welsh heritage, and worked passionately to be both Christian and Welsh, by the eighteenth century the enslavement of the Church to the English state meant that it was effectively unable to do its duty by its flock. In the nineteenth century the burgeoning impatience and cultural power of the Nonconformists, especially the Presbyterians, led to a struggle for power which led to the disestablishment of the Anglican Church in Wales. Even eighty years later the historic contamination of our church by association with social power still hangs around the Welsh Anglican Church, making it less capable than it should be of reaching out to a population alienated a long time ago. The Nonconformists claimed they were not interested in power, either social or political, but the size and grandeur of later chapel buildings suggest a rather different answer. It was a class struggle as much as a religious struggle, and it was a struggle that has left a Christian community divided, uneasy, more worried about defending its history than in getting on with the job.

Bible Study

The Temptation of Jesus
Matthew 4.1–11 (Luke 4.1–13; Mark 1.12–15)

> Jesus was led up by the Spirit into the wilderness to be tempted by the devil. He fasted for forty days and forty nights, and afterwards he was hungry. The tempter came to him and said, 'If you are the Son of God, command these stones to become loaves of bread.'
>
> But he answered, 'It is written: "Man does not live by bread alone, but on every word that comes from the mouth of God." '
>
> Then the devil took him to the holy city and placed him on the pinnacle of the temple saying to him, 'If you are the Son of God, throw yourself down; for it is written,
>
>> "He will command his angels concerning you,"
>> and "On their hands, they will bear you up,
>> so that you will not dash your foot against a stone." '
>
> Jesus said him, 'Again it is written: "Do not put the Lord your God to the test." '
>
> Again, the devil took him to a very high mountain and showed him all the kingdoms of the world and their splendour, and he said to him, 'All these I will give you if you will bow down and worship me.'
>
> Jesus said to him, 'Away from me, Satan! For it is written: "Worship the Lord your God, and serve only him." '

Then the devil left him, and suddenly angels came and waited on him.

Thus Matthew: it takes St Mark just one verse for to tell us that Jesus was tested in the desert. He is tested as the nation of Israel was tested on its escape from captivity in Egypt. St Mark says little about it other than that it happened. Matthew gives 11 verses and Luke 13 verses, as though to answer the questions: How was he tested? To what purpose? What were the issues he faced? What did he need to think through? What did he have to face before he embarked on his public ministry?

Did Jesus tell the disciples about what happened in that time of testing? He may have done, though there is no sign anywhere else of Jesus telling them anything about his own inner life. What emerge are his conclusions, not his questionings. There was no observer recording what happened and there could have been no witnesses to such events. Mark's reticence seems wise. So is this account an autobiographical account told to the disciples? That is possible, and that is how it has often been read. But, like the infancy narratives in Matthew and Luke, it could be read as an example of the kind of Jewish writing known as a midrash, a narrative with symbolic events to communicate a spiritual meaning, of how Jesus came to the conclusions and principles that he expressed to his disciples consistently through his ministry. But if Jesus spent time in the desert he could have spent time either on his own or attached to any of the many radical sects that were living out their faith and questions in circumstances of varying degrees of harshness and obsession. That could be the background to his relationship with John the Baptist. The Gospel accounts suggest that the evangelists had difficulty in describing that relationship. The issues raised in the three episodes of the temptation narrative in Matthew and Luke, whichever way you consider them, are a powerful summary of the issues that came up time and again in different forms in his encounters with the ordinary people of Israel, living under the rule of the Roman empire. They are about hunger and longing, about leadership and economics, about power, the clash of values, the struggle of what is practical in politics and public life and what it is to live under the rule of God. When read in that way they form a necessary background to decisions which Jesus makes later in his ministry, because the temptations are about what is right before God, what will meet human need, what would draw a public response. This is the basis for the ministry that is to follow, and the evangelists indicate that Jesus had it sorted out before he began his ministry. The supernatural or inner nature of the events puts the story out of reach of historical investigation – but the temptation themes are important for all Christians, for leaders and for the Church as an institution. The same issues of boundaries, power, status and ministry beset the Church today, burdened with a history more in tune with empire than subversive of it.

*   *   *

The narrative of the tempting of Jesus in the desert is modelled on what happened to the people of Israel on their escape from Egypt. They are escaping from the tyranny of Pharaoh, and their escape takes them out into the hunger and harshness of the desert, relying entirely on the provision of God. They seek a way to the promised land of milk and honey, an earthly paradise where all will be well. What better theme for a prophet thinking about leadership, the coming of the Messiah, understanding his relationship to God as sonship, in the time of another emperor, the Roman Caesar?

> The tempter came to him and said, 'If you are the Son of God, command these stones to become loaves of bread.'
>
> But he answered, 'It is written: "One does not live by bread alone, but on every word that comes from the mouth of God."'

It is from this verse in Deuteronomy that Jesus finds words to answer the challenge:

> He humbled you by letting you hunger, then by feeding you with manna, which neither you nor your ancestors were acquainted, in order to make you understand that one does not live by bread alone, but on every word that comes from the mouth of the Lord. (Deut. 8.3)

But what is this temptation about? Being hungry is not, after all, a sin. It is simply a sign of our creatureliness, our need and dependence. It is a basic human need, it is what drives our work and it is the most important in our hier- archy of needs. It is therefore an issue for all societies and their leaders and politicians. Moses had to feed the people or they would not have survived. The Caesars did it by giving out free bread as well as laying on circuses. Was Jesus contemplating a ministry which would involve an uprising by the poor and starving of the land? There was poverty enough – the story of Dives and Lazarus (Luke 16.19–31) illustrates the indifference of the Jewish rich as well as of the army to their fate. Was he being tempted to use supernatural power to change the economics of rebellion? What leader of an army would not have enjoyed feeding his troops on multiplying fish and barley loaves! There would have been no need to bother about supply lines.

When in St John's Gospel (ch. 6) Jesus feeds the five thousand there are some who want to take Jesus and make him king, at which point he vanishes from their sight. If God is there and real and ready to meet our needs why should we not make use of God for such a good, humanitarian purpose? Should we not sign him on? There are Christian traditions particularly powerful among the hungry, disempowered and marginalized that tell stories of multiplication of food (and even of petrol) in crisis situations. Like the story of the widow's curse and Elijah in 1 Kings 17, such stories illustrate the vivid faith of people who having nothing, rejoice in God's provision of enough to sustain them. People with supermarkets to titillate and satisfy their taste buds need to keep a discreet silence. In the temptation narrative, however, and in the stories of feeding the crowds, Jesus refuses to use divine power as magic for political purposes. Jesus simply quotes Deuteronomy to assert that God, the one whose very word brings us into being, is also our sustenance; there is no playing around with miracles for ulterior motives, no bypassing the imperatives of economics and history which bind ordinary mortals by supernatural power to dislodge the kingdoms of the world.

But what is the motive in the question? Is it to prove that he is the Son of God? The 'if' in the question is an 'if' of doubt. If Jesus comes to his people with God's very authority, then why should he not use the supernatural? Because our physical needs are not the most important? No, it is rather that he comes to be on the same terms as the people, as a human being, one of them – Emmanuel. Jesus comes to us, not to prove that he is supernatural, but to live out his humanity, to live as a human being relying on God. It is not in providing for the physical needs of people that Jesus will be Messiah but in dying for them.

*   *   *

> Then the devil took him to the holy city and placed him to stand on the pinnacle of the temple saying to him, 'If you are the Son of God throw yourself down; for it is written,
>
>> "He will command his angels concerning you,'
>> and "On their hands they will bear you up,
>> so that you will not dash your foot against a stone."'
>
> Jesus answered him, 'Again it is written: "Do not put the Lord your God to the test." '

The answering words of Jesus are taken from Deuteronomy:

> Do not put the Lord your God to the test, as you tested him at Massah. (Deut. 6.16)

This refers to the episode where the thirsty people demand water from Moses and where he calls on God for help.

> 'What shall I do with this people? They are almost ready to stone me.' The Lord said to Moses, 'Go on ahead of the people, and take some of the elders of Israel with you; take in your hand the staff with which you struck the Nile, and go. I will be standing there in front of you on the rock at Horeb. Strike the rock, and water will come out of it, so that the people may drink'. Moses did so in the sight of the elders of Israel. He called the place Massah and Meribah, because the Israelites quarrelled and tested the Lord, saying, 'Is the Lord among us or not?' (Exod. 17.3–7)

There is a close similarity between that question put to Moses, 'Is the Lord among us or not?' and the question put to Jesus 'If you are the Son of God'. There is an 'if' of doubt, and the question ends 'or not?' The leader who fails to meet the most basic needs of human beings for water and is faced with a riot of desperate folk is helped to discover water, and to meet their needs. Whether the event is in the desert or in a bombed city the demand for clean water is as urgent today as then. Without clean water and sanitation there is no dignified human living. Moses is able to meet that basic need, and by so doing gives proof that God is with him. Is this to save the people or to save Moses as leader? Does a leader need magical powers, to draw attention and admiration and loyalty, or does he need God with him? And what is the difference? Wonder workers draw attention to themselves and not to God. When Jesus heals or performs some 'sign' he does so out of compassion for their need not in order to prove anything about himself. This may well be why, in Mark's Gospel especially, he is constantly telling people not to tell others about what he has done. There is too his occasional impatience with the crowds of spectators, hungry for signs and wonders, and in St John's Gospel there is a clear ambivalence even about the signs. When does a sign become a stunt? Being Son of God, having God with him, is not to be exhibited in a personal quest for power or as an attractor of crowds. Attracting and pleasing crowds is the business of the spin-doctor. Crowds can be bought and sold and rented. The crowds of Palm Sunday vanish to be replaced by the rent-a-crowd of Roman power.

* * *

Again, the devil took him to a very high mountain and showed him all the kingdoms of the world and their splendour, and he said to him, 'All these I will give you if you will bow down and worship me.' Jesus said to him, 'Away from me, Satan! For it is written: "Worship the Lord your God, and serve only him."'

The answer given by Jesus is again rooted in Deuteronomy:

The Lord your God you shall fear; him you shall serve, and by his name alone you shall swear. Do not follow other gods (Deut. 6.13)

The temptation here is even more explicitly to worldly power. The offer of the kingdoms of the world depends on betraying God. The 'if' relates not to who Jesus is, but to who God is. It involves a denial of his heavenly Father. The kingdoms of the world, all their glory and splendour are to take the place of Jesus' relationship with God. It would be idolatry, with worldly power and security replacing trust in God's provision. This final temptation, like the others has to do with putting God first rather than appropriating to himself characteristics of power that belong only to God. Satan tempts Jesus to be autonomous, independent of God. That was how the snake tempted Eve and Adam. It is the temptation that constantly gnaws at human beings, the bargain that Faust accepted, it is to do things in my way, not in God's.

How did Jesus apply these principles demonstrated in the temptation story to the actions and vocation of others? Consider the story of the rich young ruler (Matt. 19.16–30; Luke 18.8–30). Here was a man coming to the boundary between spiritual and worldly power from the other side. He was an illustration of what the Jewish heritage taught that God rewards the righteous and the godly. He had sought righteousness through obedience to the commandments. He enjoyed the rewards of righteousness, the blessing of riches and earthly security. But he is not content. He has kept all the rules throughout his life, and that still leaves him with an uneasy feeling, a lack of peace in his heart about whether he is close to God or not. He asks, 'What good thing shall I do to gain eternal life?'

Jesus makes it clear that the question has to do with abandoning security, the security given by his riches, the possessions, the treasures, the status, the respect, putting all that down on the boundary between worldly success and respect on the one hand and, on the other, a total self-abandonment to living in oneness with God. The rich young ruler comes blessed with his Jewish moral heritage, the spiritual tradition of the nation, the respect of the community. He cannot let go of it – even to follow Jesus. The boundary may be narrow, but the leap of faith is too much. Jesus sees him turn his back with great sadness. It was a leap that Saul of Tarsus made, counting his inheritance as so much rubbish to win the love of Christ.

Questions

1 Unbelievers today are suspicious of believing Christians in government. Why?

2 What difficulties arise for Christians in politics today?

3 Can you be a committed and a tolerant Christian?

4 Can you be a comfortable Christian?

5 When there are arguments within the Church, for example about the place of women or the role of homosexuals, or between denominations, is the issue of power at work?

3

Peoples at the Hedge of Thorns

Once upon a time, and yet not so long ago, there lived in the bush in Australia a tribe of people uncontacted by Europeans.[1] They lived off the land using their inherited knowledge of the weather, the rocks and soil, the plants and animals to maintain a simple, hard life. They lived in harmony with their environment within a network of holy places, places made sacred by association and memory. Their chief was a good man, respected and trusted by his people, for he made wise decisions. Now it happens not infrequently that the sons of the great and the wise are a cause for concern, and this chief had a son who was wild and impetuous, hot-tempered when crossed and apparently not eager to learn wisdom. The chief and his people hoped that as he was young there was time for him to learn.

Unfortunately the chief died suddenly and according to the custom of the tribe his son became the new chief. Inheriting too soon the responsibilities of his father, the young chief showed no sign of modifying his behaviour and became even more foolish and headstrong. The people watched and worried. Their new young chief was quarrelsome and intemperate, liking to pick arguments with nearby tribes. He disregarded wise old customs and agreements on pathways and boundaries.

One day the young chief went off with his companions to

hunt. But after going some distance he felt dizzy and unwell. In no way did he wish to confess this weakness to his companions, so he announced that he was going to rest under a tree. They should go on without him and return in the evening. He settled himself under the shade of the tree and watched them go. Under the tree he slept and dreamed. Although he was a foolish young man, he knew that a dream was important and even as he slept he paid attention; when he awoke he remembered the dream and spent the day reliving the dream in his mind and thinking about what it meant.

In his dream a figure like a human being drew near to him and looked at him seriously and sadly. The figure said, 'Young man, you are not doing well. You show no sign of wisdom in leading your people. You must change your ways and become a man of peace.' The young chief felt ashamed, for indeed he knew his behaviour was a shame to his father and to himself. He knew it was a cause of fear to the people. In his dream he was ashamed and afraid. The figure of the human being said to him, 'You must change your ways. You must learn a new song which I will teach you. And you must break your spear and become a man of peace.'

So in his dream he was taught a new song and when he awoke, under the tree in the bush he sang the song over and over again until it became a part of him. When his friends returned the inner change in the young chief could be seen. He was sitting quietly, with none of the restlessness they usually found in him, so they waited for him to speak. He said, 'I slept, and in my sleep I dreamed. In the dream a figure like a human being drew near to me and looked at me seriously and sadly. The figure said to me, "Young man, you are not doing well. You show no sign of wisdom in leading your people. You must change your ways and become a man of peace." I was ashamed, for indeed I know that I have not my father's wisdom and my wildness causes shame to him. I see that my people are afraid. In my dream I was afraid and ashamed.' His young companions were astounded, for their young chief had never before admitted to fear or shame. He continued, 'The human figure said to me, "You must change your ways. You must learn a new song, which I will teach you. You must break your spear and become a man of peace." ' Then he rose and sang his new song to his friends. He took his spear and over his knee he broke it. Eventually he returned to his people and became a man of peace.

Almost a lifetime later white people from far away reached that part of Australia, and with them came teachers who were also missionaries. One day all the people gathered together to hear what the white teachers had to say. One of them spoke of a man called Jesus who came to save human beings from the effects of violence and anger and hatred. Listening under a tree in a place of honour sat the aged chief of the tribe. When the missionaries had finished, he spoke and said, 'This Saviour Jesus of whom you speak – I have already met him.' As Wali Fejo, Christian minister and native Australian, told this story to Christians from all over the world, he paused for the story to dawn in the hearts of his listeners, especially the white Christians. Then he said, 'What we ask of you is that you should look for signs of the gospel in our culture.' He paused again, and said, 'We are looking very hard for those signs in yours.'

The tale of God visiting a nomad under a tree in Genesis 18 is one of the key passages in the Old Testament. The story of the three visiting angels, who speak for 'the Lord' is sometimes referred to as 'proto-evangel' – the first glimpse of gospel to come. If God could speak to Abraham the wandering Aramean under the great oak at Mamre, could that God, in sovereign freedom, not choose to speak to a native Australian under a tree in the bush? Such starting points, such proto-gospel moments can be perceived in the folklore and traditions of many cultures all over the world. But too often they were neither looked for, nor heard. Too often the gospel came to them linked with military conquest and mercantile power.

Looking for 'signs of the gospel' in a culture was what Father Vincent Donovan of the Holy Ghost Fathers attempted when he went to live with a nomadic band of the Masai in Kenya. Disillusioned with the 'mission station' pattern of evangelism, which involved bringing nomadic people into a centre, he set out to live along with the Masai as a companion.[2] Living with them, he listened and learned, trying to pick up what were the values and cultural assumptions of the people. It was some time before they asked him why he had come, why he did not try to change their way of living as other white people had done. His answer that he had something to offer them, if they would hear him. It was a moment of great risk. They could have refused, and he was vulnerable to their decision. But their hearing of him was their choice.

A series of encounters was arranged in which the good news of Jesus was described and explored. Their response was thoughtful and profound, and there followed a teaching process in which the major issues of faith were described and discussed. Eventually the people, aware of the changes that they were embarking on, together agreed to accept and prepare for their new beginning in baptism. However, there was one individual who had only sporadically attended the teaching sessions and who seemed detached, even indifferent to what was happening. Father Vincent demurred at baptizing him. But all the others met the suggestion that he should be excluded with blank incomprehension, indeed total resistance. Their nomadic existence demanded a oneness of purpose and understanding. Either they would all become Christians, or none of them would; it was a covenant for all or for none. They belonged together.

Father Vincent gives an example of how that unity had been developed and maintained by the tribe before his arrival. He describes the process that the tribe used to bring about reconciliation after a quarrel between individuals or families. The whole group would take responsibility for caring for those who were at odds with each other. There would be a process of discussion and explanation, acceptance of responsibility and mutual apology. When the time for apology was reached, both families would prepare a special meal, and then come together. Each would eat the meal prepared by their former enemy as a sacrament of trust, forgiveness and new beginning. They knew the corrosive power of unforgiven wrong, how it could destroy the cohesiveness, the mutual understanding among them. It was a danger to their actual survival as a tribe. In that culture of united community, with this powerful process for dealing with conflict, the idea of deliberately isolating and excluding an individual for nothing more than an inadequate grasp of the content of a faith was entirely unthinkable. A faith that demanded such an approach had to be wrong. It was a moment of testing the evangelist and his message.

Father Vincent realized that while his intention was to bring gospel pure and simple, good news as empty as possible of his own cultural baggage, his 'baptism policy' was tainted by a western individualistic approach. Baptizing the whole tribe, including the individual who was in his terms inadequately prepared, was for him a revelation of what the idea of covenant with a whole people was meant to be. The evangelist learned from the evangelized.

When it came to the first celebration of the Eucharist, Father Vincent found himself up against another cultural given. Among the Masai, men and women do not eat together. It is unthinkable. But if in Christ there is no Greek nor Jew, nor male nor female, nor slave nor free, then at the Eucharist the heart of gospel says we are all alike in Christ. Therefore men and women should receive bread and wine in each other's presence because they are in the presence of Christ. Father Vincent determined that this was his sticking point. It can of course be argued that Father Vincent was undermining the culture by insisting that men and women should eat together. The first Eucharist for that tribe was new and revolutionary in that men and women ate together, but it was also rooted in their previous experience of reconciliation and the power of forgiveness. For them it was stepping out of their own culturally given situation and accepting that the gospel proclaimed something new, difficult, and revolutionary. Father Vincent and the Masai stepped together into the border land, stepped over a boundary, passed through a hedge of thorns and there found a 'pleasant place', a new creation.

In a wider context it could be pointed out that the Church that had sent Father Vincent to offer the gospel to the Masai and celebrate Eucharist with them has not even yet got around to working through the logic of its insistence that men and women should receive communion together – a logic which would make it possible for a woman to lead the celebration of the feast. Tribes that accept the gospel modify it from their own culture and assumptions. The transforming effect of gospel on culture has to be an on-going process if it is not to harden and petrify into an idol, touched by Christ, but not yet totally transformed by him.

The title of Father Vincent's book, *Christianity Redis-covered*, conveys how that re-exploring of the gospel on the boundary between cultures was a risky but transforming two-way experience. Too often we offer the gospel at no risk to our own self-understanding. When it is not simply offered but virtually enforced by military and mercantile power it is poisoned, however noble the individual mission-ary might be. That danger was spotted when missionary activity began in India and was expressed caustically by Sidney Smith, the early nineteenth-century cleric and wit, ordained in 1794, who spotted the inconsistencies very quickly.

> Let us ask too, if the Bible is universally diffused in Hindostan, what must be the astonishment of the natives to find that we are forbidden to rob, murder and steal; we who, in fifty years, have extended our empire from a few acres about Madras, over the whole peninsula, and sixty millions of people, and exemplified in our public conduct every crime of which human nature is capable. What matchless impudence to follow up such practice with such precepts! If we have common prudence, let us keep the gospel at home, and tell that Machiavelli is our prophet and the God of the Manicheans our God.[3]

This thorn hedge of cultural boundary has been there from the very beginning, because human beings fear and resist what is 'other' and different. People tend to regard what 'we' do as the 'right' way to do it and say it. The Greeks called 'barbarian' those whose language sounded like bar-bar-bar, nonsense, a barbarous babbling. But because human beings have so many things in common there is too a point of access between cultures where it is clear that whatever our differences we have experiences in common.

Such access points, such cracks or fault lines may enable a seed of the gospel to penetrate and take root. Such a moment is described in Bede's *Ecclesiastical History*.

Bede tells the story of Paulinus's proclamation of the faith to King Edwin. The king then asks his counsellors for their opinion. One of them describes their knowledge of life as being like a sparrow flying through a feasting hall, coming in from the night and returning to it. Anything which offers a better understanding of past and future must be preferred to our present ignorance. So Edwin and his counsellors accepted baptism at the hands of Paulinus. It is a vividly dramatic moment of the gospel reaching through to meet a people's need.

Within Christian traditions and practices there are myriads of variations on the idea of what a Christian community might be like. In all the nations of Europe there lie underneath the Christian layer strata of older beliefs and customs which affect the colour and shape of the later Christian community.[4] Tradition, passing on the baton, is imperceptibly modified; it adapts to secular modes of thought, economic and political forces. From time to time there are cataclysmic changes resulting from changes in the power structure.

Working on how to reach into the myriad cultures around us is the immense challenge to churches today. It is a particularly difficult challenge because what western society has is not a clearly defined culture, but a way of life in which anything goes, in which you can believe in whatever you like, picking and mixing a little bit of what you fancy for the feel-good factor. Christians often sound as if they are defending a culture rather than meeting the challenge of people's needs and terrors. The boundary where gospel changes our understanding of what it is to be human and called by God is an uncomfortable and challenging place. It is on the boundaries between our cultural heritage, the crumbling of community values, the unrestrained pressures of commercial markets that the transforming power of the gospel can create a new culture – just for our time.

So what does the future hold when the boundary is a thicket of thorns? The Welsh Quaker poet Waldo Williams asks in a poem of definitions:

> *Beth yw maddau?*   What is it, to forgive?
> *Cael ffordd trwy'r drain*   To find a way through thorns
> *at hen elyn.*   To an old enemy.[5]

Sometimes our history, long past or recent, is the thorn thicket. In the Balkans, in Ireland, in the Middle East and many others, it seems to be a totally impenetrable hedge. The massed corpses of all our wars, boundaries still littered with land mines in the ground as well as in the memory, keep us apart. So often we settle for partition and separation, wanting to have what we hold, seeing no different vision for the future. Retreating empires especially leave behind them damaged systems and poisoned relationships. Good fences might make good neighbours but boundaries run through communities in Northern Ireland – even along the way to school. Boundaries divide cultural groups and races in the great cities. New waves of immigration and settlement, of challenge and absorption – with the accompanying talk of 'being swamped' – whether in Kent, Bradford, the Lake District, the suburbs of Marseilles or in the rural heartlands of Wales – make acute demands on people, their identity and sense of security. So what does the gospel have to say in the shadow of the thorn thicket?

The faith of Israel was not a missionary faith. It did not have at its heart a command to proclaim God to the nations. At its most inclusive there was the hope that if God's people were faithful to the covenant this would in time draw the nations to God's holy hill in Jerusalem. The empires which conquered the Jews and carried them off into exile seem to have been intrigued and exasperated by the religion of this obstinate people. They warily tolerated, occasionally encouraged and more frequently tried to persecute the Jews, even to extinction. As a consequence the littleness and vulnerability of Israel has been a model of identity for many threatened people. Ironically peoples who hate each other can each perceive themselves to be God's chosen people. The instinct to guard, to resist, to be distinctive by loyalty to the covenant and to the Torah grew and was re-enacted down the centuries. This covenant loyalty, this abiding by the detail of the Torah is at its best immensely impressive and many gentiles were attracted by the moral integrity of this strange faith. There is in the gospel an individual Roman centurion who seems to have gone native, who financed the building of a synagogue and so was thought to 'deserve' to have Jesus heal his servant because 'he loves our nation'. His goodness is defined by his attitude to the community.

There is little evidence of any missionary activity from within Israel, though the Diaspora led to the formation of many synagogues outside Israel where the Jews worshipped and where 'missionaries' could have taught the essentials of the faith. It was to these that Paul initially turned to preach to Jews first of all, proclaiming Jesus as the Messiah, and it was in these places that the argument about the admission of gentiles to the earliest churches would have raged. In Matthew 24 (= Luke 11) Jesus attacks in a series of 'woes' the principles and practices of the Pharisees. One of the woes seems to suggest that Pharisees were indeed missionary in outlook:

> Woe to you scribes and Pharisees, hypocrites! For you
> cross sea and land to make a single convert, and you
> make the new convert twice as much a child of hell as
> yourselves. (Matt. 23.15)

But if the Pharisees travelled to the synagogues of the
Diaspora it would have been to persuade Jews to be
Pharisees rather than to persuade gentiles to become
observant Jews. They would have been nurturing the
scattered children of Israel and building their defences
against the surrounding cultures. They would have been
reinforcing the boundaries, not extending them. The
Pharisees began as a lay renewal movement which sought
to extend the application of the law from the priestly caste
to the laity. They laid great emphasis on cultic purity and
emphasized tithing and observance of the sabbath. This
was intended to provide a stronger sense of Jewish identity
in the face of incursions by Hellenistic culture. Jesus too
wanted a renewal of the faith of Israel, and therefore shared
some of the concerns of the Pharisees, but he was far more
concerned with the motivation of the heart. He came to be
bitterly opposed to the emphasis on cultic issues which
were external, leading to hypocrisy and imitative piety. To
the Pharisees the attitude of Jesus to the details of the Torah
would have been deeply subversive and dangerous – not
only because it diminished the importance of the law, but
also because it chipped away at the distinctiveness of the
people of Israel.

The problem with the maintenance of cultural distinctiveness is that it can hijack religion for its own purposes,
corroding religious values and diminishing our understanding of God and of what it is to be human. The story of the
Good Samaritan is not just a moral tale about the kindest
person around, but a critique of a religious system that

actually enforced upon its leaders, the priest and the Levite, behaviour that was inhuman. Jesus presents the unorthodox, despised Samaritan, who does not observe the taboos, as one who is blessedly free to behave generously and humanely. He is good precisely because he is not tied down to cultic quibbles. Jesus was not just criticizing the hypocrisy of the respectable but demolishing the very foundation of their piety. It undermined the assumptions of Jewish religious society that ensuring you were not unclean was the key to morality. The story of the Good Samaritan tells them that their religious taboos prevent them from behaving like human beings. What's more, the taboos prevent them from keeping the most basic of God's commands to love their neighbour. The neighbour is not 'people like us', but simply a person, a human being, an unnamed traveller on a desert road.

When the temple was destroyed in AD 70 Judaism naturally became even more committed to defending its identity, and the Judaism of the Pharisees became the basis of Rabbinic Judaism which had to survive without the temple sacrificial system. As in the past, in the time of Nehemiah, cultural and religious survival was focused on the Torah. This may well be the background to the bitterness of the 'woes' in the Gospels. Matthew was writing for a group of Jewish Christians who cherished their religious heritage but knew that Jesus the Messiah had been betrayed and killed for his radical criticism of its fatal flaw. The pain of letting go aspects of their cultural and religious identity was a pain that Paul had gone through after his conversion. Maintaining a religious identity was inherent to the Pharisee movement and Rabbinic Judaism, but at the same time the early Church was in the chaos of creating a new identity. Though the book of Acts seeks to present a relatively smooth progression, signs of the turmoil and bitterness of that transition remain. For the Christians – all Jews – in the joy of their new conviction that God had actually fulfilled his promises, were called to a process, which felt like betrayal. In Paul's letters, particularly in the letters to the Galatians and the Philippians, the vigour of the writing, still in the throes of the argument, conveys more immediately than the book of Acts the pain and hostility involved. The treasure of his heritage becomes for Paul 'so much rubbish' (Phil. 3.8).

The great challenge for the infant Easter Church was to move beyond Judaism, without ditching it completely. The temptation to break away completely has recurred – from the time of Marcion who wanted to set aside the Hebrew Scriptures and its crudities to contemporary ministers who claim they have never preached from the 'Old Testament'. But when St Luke cites the Song of Simeon at the story of the presentation of the infant Jesus in the temple (Luke 2.29–32), including the passage from the prophet Isaiah about being a 'light to lighten the gentiles', he is deliberately emphasizing the continuity of God's work. The song was probably already a part of the hymnody of the early Jewish Christians, expressing their joy that God had fulfilled his promises. They were accepting and owning the calling of Israel not merely to its own salvation (too small a thing) but to be the means of salvation to the non-Jewish nations, the *ethnoi*, the gentiles, indeed the whole world. The joy and explosive energy of the Easter–Pentecost experience dances in the canticles of Luke chapters 1–2. The purpose of the calling of Israel is fulfilled in Jesus.

The rest of the story, described in the book of Acts and underlying St Paul's letters, shows the cost of this radical understanding of the teaching and life and death of Jesus and of the cross and his resurrection. Having reached that understanding, Paul could not refrain from offering that salvation to the non-Jewish world. There was permanent damage as Christianity emerged from Judaism and the relationship was embittered, with all the savagery of a family quarrel. The biblical scholar James Barr describes it as the first division in the Church and the quarrel between the Jews and the Christians as an ecumenical matter. The fruit of that division is the anti-semitism that has defaced the cultures of supposedly Christian nations throughout Europe. The smoke of the Holocaust threatens the peace of the world. Today's Messianic Jews ('Jews for Jesus'), converts of American conservative evangelicals, accept that Jesus was the Messiah and attempt to build a bridge between the rejecting of Christianity of the nations and the naturally embittered resistance of Israel. Its literalist approach to the promises of the Hebrew prophets does little for the Palestinians behind concrete walls and the encroachment of settlements on the West Bank. The thorn hedge on the boundary is not a pleasant place but a place of bitterness and struggle, with accusations and counter-accusations of betrayal and injustice.

Bible Study

Acts 10.1–17

> In Caesarea there was a man named Cornelius, a centurion of the Italian Cohort, as it was called. He was a devout man and he and his whole family joined in the worship of God; he gave generously to help the Jewish people, and was regular in his prayers to God. One day about three in the afternoon he had a vision in which he clearly saw an angel of God come into his room and say, 'Cornelius!' Cornelius stared at him in terror. 'What is it,

my Lord?' he asked. The angel said, 'Your prayers and acts of charity have gone up to heaven to speak for you before God. Now send to Joppa for a man named Simon, also called Peter: he is lodging with another Simon, a tanner, whose house is by the sea.' When the angel who spoke to him had gone, he summoned two of his servants and a military orderly who was a religious man, told them the whole story, and ordered them to Joppa.

Next day about noon, while they were still on their way and approaching the city, Peter went up on the roof to pray. He grew hungry and wanted something to eat, but while they were getting it ready, he fell into a trance. He saw heaven opened, and something coming down that looked like a great sheet of sailcloth; it was slung by the four corners and was being lowered to the earth, and in it he saw creatures of every kind, four-footed beasts, reptiles and birds. There came a voice which said to him, 'Get up, Peter, kill and eat.' But Peter answered, 'No, Lord! I have never eaten anything profane or unclean.' The voice came again, a second time: 'It is not for you to call profane what God counts clean.' This happened three times, and then the thing was taken up into heaven. While Peter was still puzzling over the meaning of the vision he had seen, the messengers from Cornelius had been asking the way to Simon's house, and now arrived at the entrance.

We associate the radical change in the early Church with Paul rather than Peter, but Acts 10 tells the story of the next step in the conversion of Peter. Luke places it strategically after the description of the conversion of Saul. Paul's attempt at preaching the gospel to the Jews in Damascus proves to be utterly unfruitful. The Christians are suspicious of the zeal of the new convert and no doubt fear him as an agent provocateur. The Jews who would formerly have welcomed his help in resisting the new Christian message plot against his life. He gets no welcome back in Jerusalem; the disciples there remember the man who stood by at the stoning of Stephen, and were not entirely persuaded that he was really a disciple. Caught between the old and the new, Saul is introduced to the apostles by Barnabas, but because of his past and because he is such a controversial figure is eventually sent back home to Tarsus, leaving the Church to work its way and grow without his tempestuous presence.

There follows a time of quiet consolidation for the Christian groups before the story turns to Peter and another kind of conversion. Peter goes on a journey to Lydda and then to Joppa. He heals Tabitha and stays at the house of a tanner. As in the Gospels the geographical location of events is significant. As Peter moves out from Jerusalem he moves from conservative security to a place in which no law-abiding Jew would normally choose to live – near blood and dead animals, in the unclean stink of a tannery. If this lay on his conscience, then that unease disturbs his sleep with a dream.

The narrative switches to Caesarea – the city of the invading empire – and chapter 10 tells the story of Cornelius, 'a centurion of the Italian Cohort' who was 'a devout man who feared God with all his household; he gave alms generously to the people and prayed constantly to God' (Acts 10.2). In the story Cornelius is told about the nearness of Peter and commanded to send messengers to find him. Cornelius has been attracted by a religion which excludes him. He lives on the boundary, as close as he can, longing to belong. Like the centurion who asked Jesus to heal his servant he has been drawn to the ethic and dignity of Judaism, he has imitated the Jews as far as he can; he may even have been aware of the new movement within Judaism and in touch with what was going on. He lives as far as is possible for a Roman soldier on the border between imperial power and the spirituality of the colonial natives, he lives between official detachment and going native, and he becomes a God-fearer, an alms-giver who prays and lives as if he were Jewish. He is for Luke a symbol of the approach of the gentile to the gospel.

So we have a Roman who (unexpectedly) is a dreamer-explorer embarking upon change, meeting in his dream a figure who tells him to send for Peter, staying at the house of Simon the tanner. A Jew in a tannery must be on his way over a boundary! Meanwhile in Joppa, Peter himself has a dream/vision (Acts 10.9–22) in which a great sail descends showing him many kinds of animals which he is commanded to kill and eat. The command offends his profound cultural taboos. His protest that he has never eaten anything unclean, anything not kosher, is dismissed with the authoritative command, 'Do not call anything impure which God has made clean.' After this discomfiting message, challenging a lifetime's careful behaviour, he wakes up to be told that he is being called to visit the house of a Roman centurion. Jesus had responded to such invitations during his ministry, so Peter has a precedent, though it is not explicitly referred to.

The next day, Peter comes to the house of Cornelius and explains his presence there to the still astonished and reverent Cornelius with the words:

> 'You are well aware that it is against our law for a Jew to associate with a Gentile or visit him. But God has shown me that I should not call any man impure or unclean. So when I was sent for, I came without raising any objection.' (Acts 10.28, NIV)

That does not, it must be said, sound very enthusiastic and it is easy to miss the momentous significance and ongoing importance of the phrase 'I should not call any man impure or unclean'. He is struggling between his cultural background and the command of the Spirit. He is in the centurion's house under constraint and feels he has to make his position clear before asking what Cornelius wants. Here is Peter in no-man's-land, boundary ground, at the hedge of thorns and wondering what he is doing there. In entering the house of Cornelius he is taking the gospel into the gentile, the lawless and unclean world.

Peter's response shows him stepping his way across the boundary into the world of the gentiles and speaking with astonishment at what has happened to him. He is stepping out of the bounds of his culture, its self-definitions and taboos into a world where the assumption that God has favourites has to be challenged.

> I now realize how true it is that God does not show favouritism but accepts men from every nation who fear him and do what is right. This is the message God sent to the people of Israel, telling the good news of peace through Jesus Christ, who is Lord of all. (Acts 10.34, NIV)

Here is the dramatic moment when Peter really begins his journey over the boundary. With this step the leader of the apostles (not an upstart newcomer like Saul) brings into the burgeoning Jewish sect a painful, challenging issue that will project the faith out into the unknown and suspect world of unclean gentiles and precipitate a divide with the past. Meanwhile Saul, victim of the conservatism of observant Jews, will spend the next 14 years in Syria.

Acts 11–15 describe how the Church copes with the

crisis, for the break with Judaism is at once a triumph and a disaster which has been compounded by the hatreds of the centuries. That hostility sticks out in some of the invective against the Jews in the Gospel texts. These in their turn have served to sustain and even justify persecution of the Jews in 'Christian' Europe. The description in the book of Acts does not emphasize the difficulties and rather smoothes over the process and implies that really all was well. It is in St Paul's letter to the Galatians that we can get in touch with the anger and frustration.

In the letter to the Galatians (1.13–2.21) we learn just how bitter the argument was as conservative Jewish Christians trailed around after Paul on his missionary journeys, undoing his work, undermining his teaching and sowing doubt among the new converts. Jewish Christians believed that the new gentile Christians had to be circumcised and there were converts who seemed to be prepared to go along with that. Paul's conviction was that to accept circumcision was to accept the whole of the law, in its entirety.

Paul tells his own story in the letter to the Galatians with gathering intensity. He has to tell of the cost of his own conversion, the change from Pharisee persecutor of Christians to a new and radical freedom. From a Jewish point of view he looks like a man who has sold out on his Jewish inheritance making valueless the sacrifices of the revolt of the Maccabees. Had they suffered for nothing? Paul tells the story of his difficulties of his 14 years in Syria and Cilicia, out of sight of the Jewish congregations of Judea. He tells of his journey to Jerusalem with Barnabas and Titus to meet the disciples and Peter. The passion of that encounter, the disappointment as Peter hesitates and seems to back off from the new commitment to the gentiles is vividly described. Paul had spent the 14 years working out his understanding of the implications of the new faith. Beyond the boundaries of Israel he discovered the new radical freedom which he pronounced to the Jews and gentiles of the churches in Galatia. In Paul's understanding the coming of Christ was in order that:

> the blessing of Abraham might come to the Gentiles, so that we might receive the promise of the Spirit through faith. (Gal. 3.14)

Small wonder that he was so angry with the conservatives and so passionate in recollection of the slowness of Peter and the others to grasp the radical nature of the new and growing Church. With his conversion came his commitment to proclaim Christ to the nations, a commitment that makes him prepared to be 'all things to all people'.

> When Cephas came to Antioch, I opposed him to his face, because he stood self-condemned; for until certain people came from James, he used to eat with the Gentiles. But after they came, he drew back and kept himself separate for fear of the circumcision faction. And the other Jews joined him in this hypocrisy, so that even Barnabas was led astray by their hypocrisy. But when I saw that they were not acting consistently with the truth of the gospel, I said to Cephas before them all, 'If you, though a Jew, live like a Gentile and not like a Jew, how can you compel the Gentiles to live like Jews?' (Gal. 2.11–14)

The motive of proselytes is to get others to change to be like them. The motive of evangelists must be for converts to be like Christ. Thus our perception is that some nineteenth-century missionaries failed to distinguish in their message between what was gospel and what was their own culture. Recognizing the difference is not as easy as we presume; it demands humility in the face of a different experience of what it is to be human. The technological gulf between the world of the conqueror and the conquered was so huge that the task was fraught with difficulty. African and Indian converts had to come to Christ through the ecclesiastical and the secular culture of the missionaries, who inevitably shared much of the cultural background of the military conquerors and economic exploiters. Paul's answer in a later letter to the Corinthians provides a glimpse into his own self-understanding:

> To the Jews I became as a Jew, in order to win Jews. To those under the law I became as one under the law (though I myself am not under the law) so that I might win those under the law. To those outside the law I became as one outside the law (though I am not free from God's law but am under Christ's law) so that I might win those outside the law. (1 Cor. 9.20–21)

We catch a glimpse of the difficulty of being 'outside the law' in the behaviour of Nicodemus in the Gospel of John (chapter 3). Here is the man who is a Pharisee and moreover a member of the ruling council. He is not content with tagging along with other Pharisees to put trick questions to this remarkable new teacher, who is obviously a prophet but who might be dangerous. Nicodemus does not want to be compromised and known as the man who has actually talked to this notorious troublemaker, so he goes by night to seek out Jesus. This is indeed an intriguing scene: the insider, the establishment figure steps out in the dark towards the dangerous boundary area and the possibility of his own exclusion. The conversation between Jesus and

Nicodemus, as so often in the Gospel of John, shows how difficult it is for the conventionally minded to come to terms with a new and radical standpoint, let alone act on it. Even the disciples, who had a better chance than most to grasp what Jesus was saying, found it difficult. In the conversations with Jesus the Pharisees have an air of baffled incomprehension, for they are a group entirely convinced of the correctness of their own religious convictions, who find that they are being given dangerously 'wrong' answers. Religious discourse for them was a matter of finding out whether Jesus was orthodox, whether he was one of them, since he seemed to have much in common with them. Their questions give Jesus a chance to redeem himself, or to prove that he is wrong. It is possible in the Gospels to trace signs of the journey that Jesus himself made.

Questions

1 How would you answer Wali Fejo's challenge, 'What are the signs of the gospel in your culture?'

2 What are the cultural assumptions in the local, secular community to which you belong?

3 What is it that you don't do because of other people's expectations?

4 If you were responding to God's call for change would you start gradually or would there be a revolution in your life?

5 Peter agreed not to call anyone 'impure and profane'. Do we follow his example? What is your hedge of thorns? What are you unable to forgive?

4

Between Men and Women

The Inspector-General of Her Majesty's Hospitals in Montreal in the 1850s was an eccentric little man who rode about in a sleigh. He wore musk-ox robes and was attended by two footmen. Being Inspector-General was the highest rank available to a doctor in the army at that time, and this man's career had been a stormy one. James Barry was born in Scotland of obscure parentage and his education was sponsored by the Earl of Buchan, who was thought to be either his grandfather or his father. He trained in Edinburgh, and perhaps served as an army doctor in Spain, and Belgium; he may have been at the battle of Waterloo before going to South Africa in 1817. There he was a protégé of Lord Charles Somerset, the Governor, who declared that he was the finest doctor he had ever seen, 'but absurd in everything else'. He was the first doctor in the English-speaking world to perform a Caesarean operation.

The absurdity to which Lord Somerset referred may have arisen from the fact that James Barry was a very small man who boosted his height with three-inch soles and padded his uniform to make himself look bigger. He was said to be immensely gentle and tender with a patient in pain but very impatient with everyone else. He fought a duel, was a vegetarian, kept a goat and washed in wine. He was effeminate and bad-tempered. Barry was one of the medical officers who insulted Florence Nightingale in Scutari. When stationed in St Helena he once went off duty without permission, disappearing for months; when he returned, he told his enraged superior officer that he had been to London to have his hair cut. He retired from Montreal to London in 1864 to live with John, his black manservant, and a poodle called Psyche. When he died he was buried in Kensal Rise cemetery.

Between Barry's death and burial the woman who laid out his body discovered that this extraordinary person was in fact a woman, and as soon as the story was out, everyone said they had always suspected as much. It has been suggested that James Barry went out to South Africa to be near a man she was in love with; that was the usual explanation for women who followed armies. But this woman – whose real name we do not know – of necessity made a career for herself and got to the highest rank possible for a doctor by her skill and sheer nerve.

'James Barry', whoever she was, was only able to gain a medical education by deception, a deception sustained over the rest of her life. There are many stories of such crossings-over into male roles. These stories reveal not only the real personal resources of the individuals, but also the malice and mocking hostility of society when defined ideas about the roles of men and women are challenged, when gender boundaries are overcome. The obvious biological differences between men and women become the basis for educational, cultural and economic constraints and discrimination which have amounted to oppression and persecution. An educated woman not under the authority of a man had to be suspected of immorality. There are myths of origin in most cultures which offer explanations as to why gender differences exist, and they work not only to explain but to justify and sustain the differences, maintaining the boundaries.

That is the way in which the myth of Adam and Eve has long sustained the subjection of women to men. The Christian Church began with a remarkable vision of a community in which there might be equality, in which being Jew or Greek, free or slave, male or female did not matter. But it was a community whose roots were deep in the Judaic tradition, and it had to compromise to survive in Graeco-Roman society, both elements of which were essentially patriarchal. Often religious systems which begin with a new vision of the common humanity of men and women slide back into patriarchal assumptions. It is extraordinary that, despite the persistence of theologically sustained misogyny, men and women have still managed to live together and love, finding joy and holiness on the delightful boundary of difference between them. Nevertheless, change has been in the air for a while. There are passages in the New Testament epistles which our present-day lectionaries either omit or put in square brackets because they are too embarrassing to be read aloud to modern congregations.

Perhaps it takes someone whose cultural background is genuinely diverse, who is still in touch with different myths of origin, to describe the comedy and tragedy of the way in which men and women behave within arbitrary patterns and rules. Louise Erdrich is a poet and novelist whose early novels describe the lives of contemporary Native American people. She grew up in North Dakota and is of Native American and European descent, enrolled in the Turtle Mountain Band of Ojibwe. She also has German ancestors, and like many Americans is intrigued by the process of exile and home-making in a new world, when different peoples and cultures mix and how this works out from one generation to the next. In *Love Medicine* she describes reservation life; not merely the poverty and frustration, but the loss of clarity and understanding. She describes people of mixed race and background, the way in which this can sometimes produce a rich creativity, at other times only contradiction and sterility. Another major theme in her work is the effect on native culture and religion of Christian mission (both Lutheran and Catholic) allied to white domination and economic oppression.

This is evident in her intriguing, if cumbersomely titled, novel *The Last Report on the Miracles at Little No Horse*.[1] It is about a Roman Catholic priest, Father Damien Modeste, who has lived among the Ojibwe for more than half a century. His missionionary organization had long ago established a church among the Ojibwe, together with a convent. The impact of a florid nineteenth-century Catholic spirituality, with its huge stress on sainthood and miracles, produced a society in which native perceptions of the good, the true and the beautiful were distorted, in which the depth and breadth of Catholic faith was only partially understood and aspired to. Openness to the spiritual and the supernatural becomes an unbalanced searching for the miraculous. Hence a damaged young woman becomes a focus for 'miraculous' events and healings and the community wants its own attested 'saint' formally recognized by Rome. The economic context is of extreme poverty afflicting a people disrupted by loss and change.

Part of the hilarity and agony of the story is that Father Damien is really a woman! The first part of the novel tells how the young Agnes de Witt, stripped of all she possessed, even her clothes, by storm, flood and banditry, arrives among the Indians dressed in a cassock. Agnes has already had a complex history before her change of role; she had been a nun, sister Cecilia, whose German inheritance is a deep love of music. Cast out on her own through various deeply traumatic adventures, including a passionate love affair, stripped to her skin by storm and flood, she takes the cassock of a dead priest on his way to minister to the Ojibwe; her motive in doing so is simply to defend herself against rape. Making herself in this way untouchable she successfully plays the priestly role, and then has to keep up the pretence. The people accept her for what she looks like, a slight, frail, effeminate priest – not at all unusual. The structure of the institution and what is expected of its priests both sustains and constrains her, so she plays the part initially reluctantly and then more confidently as the years roll by. Her Christian faith and experience make her acutely aware of the disgraceful, even blasphemous nature of her deceit, but she is unable to extricate herself without causing even more damage than by soldiering on. She is frightened, not so much of being found out, but by the fact that the invalidity of her ministry would be perceived as eternally damaging to all the people she has loved and ministered to. You may ask how can institutional rules and regulations declare love and service invalid? Ask the validly ordained but married Roman Catholic priests of Czechoslovakia, who lived under communist oppression during the Cold War.

The narrative tells of a campaign to have Sister Leopolda, a partly Indian woman whose real name is Pauline Puyat, declared a saint; it brings into the community an ecclesiastical bureaucrat who by his enquiries disturbs the fragile balance of the community and threatens Father Damien's secret. Father Damien knows in her heart that Sister Leopolda had no inkling of the nature of holiness. But disclosing the truth would reveal to the authorities the untruth of Father Damien. At one level the novel is a sardonic response to Roman Catholic ecclesiastical culture and structure. But it is far more than that, for it celebrates the transforming potential of sexual discovery and self-giving, the spiritual power of music and liturgy. It describes true priesthood serving the marginal, the forgotten and excluded; it shows too how the power of evil corrodes and destroys. The convoluted story with its hilarious ironies is told with passion, gentleness and great verve. The boundaries between male and female, lay and ordained, Indian and white, native spirituality and Christian doctrine mix in this melting pot to become a chaos at once ridiculous, exhilarating and tragic. The ambiguity of people's motives and understandings, their wounds and loss are richly conveyed. The story is resolved – if at all – in the relationship between Father Damien and Nanapush, the Indian shaman. They listen to each other, and reach a space on the boundary between their faith and culture in which a mutual recognition of integrity takes place; they find an area of common challenge and comfort. Even in chaos the brooding Spirit can be recognized.

These words of Nanapush are quoted at the beginning of the work:

There are four layers above the earth and four layers below. Sometimes in our dreams and creations we pass through the layers, which are also space and time. In saying the word *nindinawemaganidok*, or, all my relatives, we speak of everything that has existed in time, the known and the unknown, the unseen, the obvious, all that lived before or is living now in the worlds above and below.

In her novel cultures are laid open to judgement; Erdrich challenges us to discover what truth the gospel has to offer from that chaotic detritus. What is there to say about maleness and femaleness, about white domination and genocide, about native vulnerability and complicity? In her last brooding sermon, distilled out of her journey and her pain, Father Damien asks, 'What is the whole of our existence but the sound of an appalling love?'

That 'appalling love' of which Father Damien speaks is a striking concept for cross-bearing Christians; it conveys something of the driving force which has sustained her technically fraudulent priesthood. She is trapped on the boundary by expectations, yet her true self achieves an entirely uncanonical holiness despite the fraud.

Gender appears basic to our sense of personhood. The first question asked when a child is born is 'Is it a boy or girl?' We seem to need to know the gender of the new person before we can even begin to think about or relate to her/him. Maleness and femaleness seem to determine not only who we are, but how we behave to other people. In traditional societies the boundaries between men and women are set down clearly; the distinction between the nest-maker and the hunter-gatherer, the child-bearer and the warrior are abundantly clear. Yet the sheer variety of ways in which men and women have ordered their lives together and apart is evidence that this is something we rarely get right. Sometimes what we perceive as the difference between men and women is just a variant on the difference between persons and their otherness to each other. It is significant too that myths of origin, whether in Genesis or in Native American tradition, apportion great importance to the relationship between the sexes.

The Christian doctrine of the Fall, seeking to explain the mess of sin in which humanity is entrapped, is a story about the relationship between a man and a woman. The first evidence of a breakdown in the relationship with God is a breakdown in the relationship between Adam and Eve, between dust and life. Our myth of origin has been used to enforce the subordination of women ever since. The distortion of the relationship between men and women, our infinite capacity for getting the relationship wrong, the power of patriarchy – all have used the myth to justify withholding education from girls, for depriving them of property, for removing their individuality and autonomy as individuals, leaving them defined as daughters, mothers, wives. As Milton described Adam and Eve: 'He to God only, she to God in him.' Not good news.

A Navaho myth of origin, 'The River of Separation' offers a lively, and slightly bawdy comment on gender difference. At first, as in Eden, men and women live together successfully and co-operatively: the men hunt, the women gather, all are well-fed and – so the story implies – enjoy a vigorous sex life. One day in her home, her *hogan*, a woman leans back after a good meal and, patting her private parts, says (in a translation more respectable than the original would sound to our ears), 'Thank you, my womanhood.' Her husband is outraged. He leads his fellow males across the nearby river to live apart; the river immediately becomes impassable. Neither sex has to bother with adapting to meet the other's needs; they can live as they like. But eventually the women find that life without meat is poor, while the men cannot keep house. Moreover, no more children have been born. Shouting to each other across the river, the two sides make up their quarrel, the river becomes passable, and they live together once more.

Myths, cultures, art, music, drama, dance, religious activity are all rooted in the conflicts and passionate obsessions of men and women with each other. Shakespeare describes it in *The Taming of the Shrew*. We are less familiar with a riposte to Shakespeare written by John Fletcher called *The Tamer Tamed*[2] in which the widowed Petrucchio is hilariously overcome by his second wife. The play's epilogue declares that the aim of the story is:

To teach both sexes due equality,
and as they stand bound to love mutually.

But our inability to get this relationship right, complicated by issues of power and violence is still at the heart of the mess: in the Aids disaster in Africa, in unfed and uneducated girl children in India, in the shocking gender imbalance in China, in the traffic of women from eastern to western Europe. Adam and Eve, Cain and Abel – the myths still speak for us.

Where then, if we dismiss the model of female submission, do we find help in God's word on this particular boundary? Is there anything in the Christian Scriptures indicating a gospel way of looking at human society and the relationship between men and women? Some interpreters note in St Luke's Gospel an enlightened interest in the women around Jesus and his attitude to them. Others argue that, on the contrary, Luke is intent upon presenting portraits of docile and submissive women.

Issues of gender boundaries were familiar to Jesus. His own religious culture certainly confined the role of women. We don't know whether Jesus ever heard the prayer, which later rabbis used, thanking God for not having been born a woman. He seems to have paid scant attention to the meticulous rules of taboo which the law laid down to ensure the separation of men and women. Just as he seems not to have been bothered about the details of sabbath-keeping and handwashing, neither did he bother about what people thought of his talking to women, having women touch him, having them break into men-only groups or behaving emotionally and extravagantly.

St Luke tells of women who travelled with the disciples and supported them financially. They were not a group of beggars. But there were no women among the Twelve.

What was the significance of the fact that Twelve are recognized as 'the Apostles'? Was it simply the use of a special number, like 3 or 40 or 70, not arithmetical but symbolic? Certainly it reminded people of the foundation of the people of Israel by the 12 patriarchs, sons of Jacob/Israel. What was the difference between being one of the Twelve and being one of the other disciples? The women in the Gospels seem to be disciples in fact if not in name. But rabbis just did not have women disciples. Women did not study Torah.

As well as the supportive women, there are many stories of Jesus meeting with women marginalized for various reasons: Mary Magdalene 'healed of seven demons', the Samaritan woman at the well, the woman caught in adultery. There are stories of women understanding things sooner than the men, who are often presented as unperceptive and rather dim. It is the women who care lovingly for the tired, hungry and dejected Jesus. It is a woman who anoints his head, recognizing his kingship, anointing him before his suffering. Her name will be remembered, says Jesus, not taking into account the way in which male groups diminish women and forget their names; the evangelist doesn't mention the name that Jesus wanted remembered. So we will consider two other episodes in which religious gender taboo and the boundaries between men and women are significant.

Bible Study

The daughter of Jairus and the bleeding woman
Mark 5.21–43 (Luke 8.40; Matt. 9.18–26)

When Jesus had crossed again in the boat to the other

side, a great crowd gathered around him; and he was by the sea. Then one of the leaders of the synagogue named Jairus came and, when he saw him, fell at his feet and begged him repeatedly, 'My little daughter is at the point of death. Come and lay your hands on her, so that she may be made well and live.' So he went with him.

And a large crowd followed him and pressed in on him. Now there was a woman who had been suffering from haemorrhages for twelve years. She had endured much under many physicians, and had spent all that she had; and she was no better, but rather grew worse. She had heard about Jesus and came up behind him in the crowd and touched his cloak, for she said, 'If I but touch his clothes, I will be made well.' Immediately her haemorrhage stopped; and she felt in her body that she was healed of her disease. Immediately aware that power had gone forth from him, Jesus turned about in the crowd and said, 'Who touched my clothes?' And his disciples said to him, 'You see the crowd pressing in on you; how can you say, "who touched me?" ' He looked all around to see who had done it. But the woman knowing what had happened to her, came in fear and trembling, fell down before him, and told him the whole truth. He said to her, 'Daughter, your faith has made you well; go in peace, and be healed of your disease.'

While he was still speaking, some people came from the leader's house to say, 'Your daughter is dead. Why trouble the teacher any further?' But overhearing what they said, Jesus said to the leader of the synagogue, 'Do not fear, only believe.' He allowed no one to follow him except Peter, James and John, the brother of James, When they came to the house of the leader of the synagogue, he saw a commotion, people weeping and wailing loudly. When he had entered, he said to them, 'Why do you make a commotion and weep? The child is not dead but sleeping.' And they laughed at him. Then he put them all outside, and took the child's father and mother and those who were with him, and went in where the child was. He took her by the hand and said to her, 'Talitha cum,' which means, 'Little girl, get up!' And immediately the girl got up and began to walk about (she was twelve years of age). At this they were overcome with amazement. He strictly ordered them that no one should know this, and told them to give her something to eat.

Jesus has just returned over the lake from the region of the Gerasenes where he has healed a demon-possessed man. He returns to his own land to encounter a request from a pillar of the community, a ruler of the synagogue whose 12-year-old daughter is very ill, apparently dying. Here Jesus, the radical rabbi, whose reputation as a healer has made him famous, is asked for help by someone entirely respectable, someone who has responsibility for leading the observant religious life of the community and for the obedience of individuals to the demands of the law. Here Jesus is surely safe within his own tradition and community and culture. He is teaching the people beside the lake when the man comes, casts himself at his feet and asks for help. 'My little daughter is dying. Please come and put your hands on her so that she will be healed and live.' No questions are asked; Jesus just goes with him.

On the way, surrounded by a jostling crowd, someone who is an outcast of that society, who had no business to be among people, in her desperation comes close to him hoping that merely touching his clothing will heal her. Here is the woman who had been subject to bleeding for 12 years; she has been excluded and regarded as unclean during the whole lifetime of the little girl whom Jesus is going to see. The ruler of the synagogue, loving father though he clearly was, would certainly have excluded her. Jewish law and cultural custom declared women unclean for seven days of each month. Abnormal constant or irregular bleeding would have made her permanently unclean.[3] Some commentators will argue that 'uncleanness' was not a category that had moral connotations, that it did not mean 'dirty'; it was 'ritual' uncleanness, a technicality in a system devised for the health of the community. But the effect on the individual was to be excluded, and that had practical, economic effects; it would affect all social intercourse, and it would certainly affect the individual psychologically with an acute version of what is blandly called 'low self-esteem'. The leprosy and skin disease laws worked in the same way – but normal menstruation is not a disease or a malfunction. A woman with a normal menstrual cycle could not avoid the monthly experience of exclusion and being regarded as impure. Blood itself, containing 'life', was taboo. But this woman, brave in her desperation, comes forward and deliberately touches the clothing of a rabbi. She must have heard that here was a rabbi unlike other rabbis, unlike rulers of synagogues, unlike the scruple-mongers and fundamentalist sticklers for the law.

The bleeding woman has the same kind of faith as the ruler of the synagogue. He believed that Jesus could heal his daughter, she believes that Jesus will heal her. He has status and is able to meet Jesus man to man. The unclean woman comes up secretly, hiding her 'impurity' but wanting her debilitating sickness healed. She breaks the rule that no unclean woman should touch anyone, let alone a holy man. She risks making him unclean – perhaps touching his cloak wouldn't count but would be enough to heal her.

Jesus perceives the significance of this one touch in the middle of a jostling crowd. There is the moment of his knowing the meaning of the touch, and of her knowing that her bleeding has stopped and 'she felt in her body that she was freed from her suffering'. At the same moment 'Jesus realized that power had gone out from him'. This phrase is not repeated by Matthew and Luke, perhaps because of the idea of Jesus' healing power being automatic or limited. But the absurdity of asking who had touched him is evident. Equally absurd is the idea that Jesus is made unclean by contact with a woman and that this cultural taboo makes sense. Jesus persists in looking over the crowd to see who it might be. It is then that the woman realizes that there is more to be healed than merely the haemorrhaging. She, like the leader of the synagogue, falls at his feet to confess. She has broken a rule and therefore has to confess. There is, however, no word of complaint from Jesus. No protest that he has been made impure by her touch, no telling her to go home and keep out of the way of the clean, no suggestion that anything untoward has happened. Simply her faith and her touching him has brought about her healing; that healing is not magical, because a relationship is established.

This for women is one of the most powerful stories in the Gospels. Male commentators do not seem to be touched by its implications. Menstruation is taboo in most societies. It is mysterious, female, other, 'unclean'. In the Orthodox churches, clearly inheritors of Jewish attitudes in this as in some other matters, there was a canon that no menstruating woman might receive communion. It is claimed that such a canon is no longer operative. Perhaps not, in the West. But isn't it clear that something very odd is happening when an exclusively male priesthood, involved in a ritual in which wine acquires the significance of blood and life everlasting, excludes women because they are bleeding? A biological feature is made a taboo which excludes and disempowers.

Menstruation, even in our society, was until very recently almost unmentionable, and is still not normally discussed in mixed society. In the early part of the twentieth century it was effectively as taboo as in Jewish society. Chad Varah founded the Samaritans after an occasion when a girl of 13 in his parish committed suicide. Experiencing her first menstrual period, not knowing what was happening to her, she thought she was suffering from a terrible disease and was too ashamed to tell anyone. Such ignorance and shame were not uncommon. The sick girl in the Scripture is slightly younger, 12 years old. It might be significant, for she is at the age of moving from childhood to puberty, from innocence to incipient sexuality; she is on the verge of womanhood. Jesus' journey to her is delayed by having to deal with this outcast woman who has been ill for as long as the girl has lived. Then messengers arrive saying the little girl has died.

So Jesus moves on to deal with another taboo – death. Dread of contact with a dead body is at the root of Jesus' critique of his own culture in the story of the Good Samaritan where the demands of ritual cleanness for the priest and the Levite make them behave in a way that is deeply inhumane. Jesus clearly does not share that dread, for he continues on his way to the home of the ruler of the synagogue. He is already unclean from his contact with the sick woman, yet he risks further uncleanness through contact with a dead child. There is also a mysteriousness about whether the child is dead or not. Hanging over the story is the fear that delay with the haemorrhaging woman has allowed an innocent child to die. Jesus' response both to the respectable and the unclean is the same. He responds with humanity to their need, unconstrained by barriers of religion, gender or culture. He heals within his relationship to a real person, whether it be an authoritative but needy father, an unclean woman or a dying child.

The purpose of religious taboo is a complicated and deeply rooted cultural issue which is responsible for much misunderstanding between groups. What is taboo ranges from gravely offensive to milder things that are 'not done', but give people occasion for disapproving of each other both socially and morally. While some taboos have a utilitarian source which westerners can countenance, the issues of clean and unclean, of in and out, of acceptable to God and unacceptable to God, are difficult to understand.

For Jews the advisability or beneficial effect of a taboo was not, and is not, the issue. If God has commanded or forbidden something, the issue is one of obedience, not of benefit. This applies to circumcision, the uncleanness rules, the food taboos, the washing rules. Such obedience has the effect of defining the community which belongs to God, holy, sacred, separate from the unclean outsiders. The use of an *eruv* – a visible cord defining the home ground of an orthodox Jewish community – sustains that law-abiding culture to this day in some of the great cities of the West.

As a matter of courtesy to a culture, especially a culture that has been driven through the gas chambers, we need to be very careful about how we express our reservations. Taboo clearly has a protective and self-defining function. It has a certain attraction. But certainly one of the results of this use of taboo is to perceive those 'without the law' as unclean. They are the gentiles. In Matthew 15.1–28 Jesus moves into the world outside his own religion and culture.

The Canaanite woman and her daughter
Matthew 15.1–28

Then Pharisees and scribes came to Jesus from Jerusalem and said, 'Why do your disciples break the tradition of the elders? For they do not wash their hands before they eat.' He answered them, 'And why do you break the commandment of God for the sake of your tradition? For God said, "Honour your father and your mother," and "Whoever speaks evil of father or mother must surely die." But you say that whoever tells father or mother, "Whatever support you might have had from me is given to God," then that person need not honour the father. So, for the sake of your tradition, you make void the word of God. You hypocrites! Isaiah prophesied rightly about you when he said:

"This people honours me with their lips,
   but their hearts are far from me;
in vain do they worship me,
   teaching human precepts as doctrines." '

Then he called the crowd to him and said to them, 'Listen and understand: it is not what goes into the mouth that defiles a person, but it is what comes out of the mouth that defiles.' Then the disciples approached him and said to him, 'Do you know that the Pharisees took offence when they heard what you said?' He answered, 'Every plant that my heavenly Father has not planted will be uprooted. Let them alone; they are blind guides of the blind. And if one blind person guides another, both will fall into a pit.' But Peter said to him, 'Explain this parable to us.' Then he said, 'Are you also still without understanding? Do you not see that

whatever goes into the mouth enters the stomach, and
goes out into the sewer? But what comes out of the
mouth proceeds from the heart, and this is what defiles.
For out of the heart come evil intentions, murder,
adultery, fornication, theft, false witness, slander. These
are what defile a person, but to eat with unwashed hands
does not defile.'

Jesus left that place and went away to the district of Tyre
and Sidon. Just then a Canaanite woman from that
region came out and started shouting, 'Have mercy on
me, Lord, Son of David; my daughter is tormented by a
demon.' But he did not answer her at all. And his
disciples came and urged him saying, 'Send her away, for
she keeps shouting after us.' He answered, 'I was sent
only to the lost sheep of the house of Israel.' But she came
and knelt before him, saying, 'Lord, help me.' He
answered, 'It is not fair to take the children's food and
throw it to the dogs.' She said, 'Yes Lord, yet even the
dogs eat the crumbs that fall from their masters' table.'
Then Jesus answered her, 'Woman, great is your faith!
Let it be done for you as you wish.'

Here we come to a key chapter in which Matthew the Jew,
writing for Jewish Christians, retelling the story of Jesus the
Jew, struggles with the issue of ritual cleanness. It all begins
with the issue of the washing of hands. The scrupulous
Pharisees, offended several times over by Jesus, send a
deputation to discuss some carelessness on the part of the
disciples who have clearly not kept all the required rules.
Jesus does not even attempt to answer the accusation.
Clearly the conversation has begun in truculent fashion
because he gets his retaliation in quickly by asking another
question which clearly says in effect, 'Why worry about

that kind of detail when you're not keeping much more important laws?' Jesus goes back to the ten commandments, to the basic 'Honour your father and your mother'. This human responsibility to care for and honour parents is contrasted with using the later tradition of the elders, to get out of that responsibility. It is another example of giving a higher priority to 'religious' obligations than to humane and loving relationships. Just as the priest and the Levite in the story of the Good Samaritan are constrained by the law of uncleanness to behave in an inhumane way, so demands made by the religious system on money can give people an excuse for not dealing with their primary responsibility for their families. Jesus challenges the tradition where it undermines humane behaviour and the purpose of God.

Jesus was not the first to do this. Indeed he follows in the prophetic tradition of casting and recasting the story of the relationship of Israel with God. Religious systems are in this sense self-serving, dragging people into religious rather than to serving activity. The prophets are constantly reassessing this kind of hierarchy of importance. The prophet Jeremiah, at a time of radical reform of temple worship in the reign of King Josiah, denounces a people who cannot see the difference between the letter of the law and the love of God and neighbour.

Do not trust in deceptive words and say, 'This is the temple of the Lord, the temple of the Lord, the temple of the Lord!' If you really change your ways and your actions and deal with each other justly, if you do not oppress the alien, the fatherless or the widow and do not shed innocent blood in this place and if you do not follow other gods to your own harm, then I will let you live in this place, in the land I gave to your forefathers for ever and ever. (Jer. 7.4–7)

There is in the Old Testament a clear struggle with this issue, and Jesus at this point is acting out his instruction, 'You have heard it said by the men of old, but I tell you . . .' Like Jeremiah, Jesus embarks on a sweeping denunciation of concern over ritual and taboo rules which make it difficult to keep the humane heart of the Torah. What is the point of keeping little rules if our hearts are far from God? He quotes another of the radical prophets:

> These people honour me with their lips,
> but their hearts are far from me.
> They worship me in vain;
> their teachings are but rules taught by men. (Isa. 29.13)

There follows what seems to be a thorough cancelling of the dietary laws. It is not what we put into our mouths that makes us unclean, but rather the spoken words that come out. The disciples are disconcerted and point out to Jesus that the Pharisees are offended by his words. Jesus confirms their unease by dismissing the rules as plants that God has not planted and the scrupulous Pharisees as mere blind guides who will lead the people into a pit. Matthew, writing for Jewish Christians, knows that the meticulous keeping of rules is still the instinct and probably custom of his community, the instinct to exhibit holiness and keep a score of righteousness is active within his congregation. The tendency to keep religious, cultic, dietary, cultural rules is active in all human groups, and the growth of religious fundamentalisms of all kinds flourishes on this tendency, which Jesus challenges, not only in the Pharisees, but in his own disciples. The Gospel writer is reminding his own community of this.

Peter asks for an explanation of the parable, so Jesus expands the metaphor, pointing out that food is food; it is taken in and is passed out of the body as faeces into the sewer. It is just matter, stuff, end of story. That is how our bodies work and are sustained. Evil is from deeper inside us, and it is out of our heart that come thoughts and subsequent acts of murder, fornication, stealing. These are the great moral issues, these are what make us unclean, not fussing about scruples and washing up (this of course at a time when no one understood the connection between handwashing and food poisoning).

The episode seems to show Jesus in exasperation with the minutiae of the law when the human heart is unable to be obedient to God's will for humanity. It seems that the evangelist is setting a context for the next story in which Jesus crosses another set of boundaries. First he does so physically by leaving Israel proper and withdrawing to the region of Tyre and Sidon. It is as if he has had a bellyful of legal nit-picking in his own religious culture; but he realizes that his own critique offends not only the Pharisees but makes his own disciples uneasy as well. They know the rules, they feel safe within them. Questioning the cultural rules that have a religious provenance even if they seem pointless, make people insecure. So Jesus 'withdraws' and crosses a political and religious boundary, beyond Israel.

Whether this was the order of events we do not know, but this is how the evangelist-editor chooses to highlight the issue. Jesus goes out of Israel to get some fresh air, presumably hoping for some peace and quiet. But human needs await him beyond Israel. He finds that his fame has gone before him, and he is almost immediately pestered by a Canaanite woman from that vicinity who calls out to him, addressing him by his noble Jewish title of 'Son of David', and pleads for her daughter who is possessed by a demon. The very idea that the impure Canaanites might have a claim on him exasperates the disciples. Not for the first time they beg Jesus to send someone needy away. In Jewish terms she is beyond the pale. She comes from beyond the boundary of Israel, she is not one of the lost sheep of the house of Israel. She is a Canaanite, a woman, and has no right to anything. she is another pestering woman, therefore, say the disciples, 'Send her away.'

The following scene has caused much embarrassment since it appears at first sight that Jesus shares his disciples' approach; his attitude could be described in modern terms as xenophobic.

> I was sent only to the lost sheep of Israel . . . It is not fair to take the children's food and throw it to their dogs.

Did he say really that? Did he mean it, or rather, what did he mean? Does it simply mean that this was how at this point he had been thinking about his ministry? Or does it express his own frustration with the nit-pickers? Is there irony here, even self-mockery here? There are various ways in which to explain it away, to modify and reinterpret it to remove the scandal and make it acceptable. The suggestion that we should translate as *puppies* rather than *dogs* does not deal adequately with the apparent offence.

For minorities and abused peoples there is no great difficulty in saying that the Canaanite woman teaches Jesus a lesson. You can simply accept that Jesus comes from his own human culture prejudiced against her both as a woman and as a Canaanite. He treated the outcast and an 'unclean' Jewish woman with courtesy. Would he behave in such an unfeeling way to a suffering woman and her child, just because they were foreigners? It doesn't seem like Jesus. Nor does it seem like Jesus to believe he is simply putting this woman to some sort of test.

A great Baptist preacher from the southern United

States, the Revd Jack Jones, preached on this story during a World Council of Evangelism conference in Salvador Bahia in 1996. He beamed with delight. 'I *love* this woman!' he proclaimed, 'She *argues* with the Lord.' Jack Jones's black people had had to argue with an interpretation of Scripture that told them to obey their masters when they were slaves because Paul had told Roman slaves to do so. But the black slaves of the southern United States took their Bibles out to the cotton fields and learnt to interpret the text themselves; they argued their way into their own relationship with the God of the white, slave-owning masters. They learned to search the Scriptures for words which would be for them the word of God, like 'Tell Pharaoh to let my people go.' They turned it into song, a subversive and dangerous song of challenge and hope. A people of that experience are instinctively on the side of the Canaanite woman. 'I love this woman – she argues with the Lord.' Here, insisted Jack Jones, is Jesus learning, growing out of the inherited racism and sexism of his own culture.

Homosexual people, struggling to live according to their own sexual orientation, are involved in our day in a similar process of 'arguing with the Lord'. The Lord himself seems not to have said anything on the subject, but they, like slaves and women, have to tussle with intransigences in the texts, and deeply entrenched attitudes in the institution.

Those unwilling to accept that Jesus might be in any way limited by his specific humanity, his male Jewishness, are uneasy with such a straightforward approach. But if you read this episode as a continuation of the argument about washing cups in the first 21 verses of the chapter, then this is one step in the argument that Jesus has been having with his own tradition and the people who enforce it. The debate matters, not because the Pharisees criticize the disciples, but because it has to do with real suffering humanity. It is not a past conflict between Jews and gentiles that is at stake, but the conflicts of people today who declare that other nations don't matter, whether they be Bosnians, Croats, Serbs, Roma, Albanians, Iraqis, Kurds, Iroquois, Hutus and Tutsis, Maori, Aborigine. The impure are any 'them' who are different from 'us', especially sojourners who belong nowhere.

Another view is possible, if not provable. The words of the text of the New Testament never say whether Jesus is smiling, ironically or otherwise. If Jews winked then perhaps he even winked at this moment? He knows she knows what the situation is. She can see the annoyance on the faces of the disciples. She knows who he is – she has just called him 'Lord! Son of David'. She is acknowledging that here is a great Jewish leader; the Jews had never done much for the Canaanites, but at least this one is talking to her – and she a woman! She acknowledges his power and so she presses her case, since what matters is not Jewish suscepti-bilities but getting her daughter healed. Might this leader have compassion on her? Jesus may be conveying to her – between the lines so to speak – something like this: 'You know that the rules don't allow me to do anything for you. I thought I could work *within* the rules. You are showing me that I can't.'

This interpretation makes it possible to accept that Jesus is struggling precisely with this issue. He has passed over the physical boundary of Israel. Will he now pass over the cultural, religious and gender boundaries and heal someone who is not 'one of us'? For whom is his mission? Is the good news really only for the lost sheep of the house of Israel, those who belong to us? Stepping out of Israel he meets a brave woman with a sick daughter. He learns to listen to her plea for help as he listened to fathers of sick daughters in Israel. His response to sickness has always been to heal out of compassion, and out of a relationship with the sick person. That same human compassion works in him beyond the boundary as he argues either with himself or with her. She becomes the champion of all excluded races and cultures as well as of her downtrodden sex. In the process we see Jesus shedding a cultural chrysalis and stepping out over a boundary to heal.

To the words of Jesus, words reminding her that she knows as well as he does that the non-Jews are 'dogs', she replies 'even the dogs eat the crumbs that fall from the master's table'. Would it help to know what was the expression on her face, and what the expression on Jesus' face. Was he ashamed? Was he laughing at himself, even apologizing for the arrogance of the language? Was he making fun of the way in which human groups speak in derogatory fashion of frogs, pakis, niggers, yids? Perhaps he had just learned a lesson. He was showing to his disciples how to cross the boundary from an exclusive nation into a broader humanity.

The story as told would have had a powerful resonance for the Jewish–Christian community of Matthew the evangelist. They too were on the boundary between their own cultural and religious identity on the one hand, and on the other hand the new world of this gospel in which they are to fulfil the prophecy of Isaiah that they will be a light to lighten the gentiles.

Questions:

1 What in your society do women not do? Why not?

2 What is it men don't do? Why not?

3 Are these distinctions God-given?

4 Do gender constraints enable men and women to grow in faith and love?

5 What is the value of 'custom of the elders'?

6 What value of the elders does your community/ family need to drop?

7 What boundaries do you think you have crossed as a woman or as a man?

5

Communicating and Language

It was March 1825 in the Aleutian Islands of Alaska, then part of the Tsarist empire. It was Easter and the Orthodox missionary Father John Veniaminov had for the first time since his arrival celebrated the liturgy of Pascha. He had processed around his church, proclaiming that 'Christ is risen from the dead, trampling down death by death!', going through the ancient rite in his traditional Russian-style vestments. Later in the morning he went from one native yurt to another with the proclamation that 'Christ is risen'. Father John noticed that there seemed to be a real 'spirit of Pascha' around. His parishioners, who had struck him from the first as curiously impassive, were all in notice-ably cheerful mood. Could they really have been so touched by this first celebration of the resurrection? This first celebration had been of course in Church Slavonic, mysteriously numinous to Russians but incomprehensible to the Aleuts. What Father John had discovered was that his flock were responding to the most basic of the joys of the year. The month of March in Aleut is Kisagunak, which means simply 'We have things to eat'. The returning light and the rising temperature meant they had been able to get out to hunt, to replenish their stocks of food and to feast. During winter they had had no choice but to be hungry. Fasting was not a chosen exercise for spiritual reasons but a harsh unavoidable fact of life. They would now, more in the spirit of play than commercial profit, think about complying with demands from the Russian traders that they go out and do some hunting for skins.

Father John Veniaminov was not slow to appreciate such dovetailing of human emotions across cultural boundaries. He had quickly learned to respect the ways and skills of the native Aleuts in surviving the hardships of the climate. Additionally he had accepted an equally difficult challenge – learning the Aleut language, enabling him to open a school for 22 village children. By January 1826 he was translating a catechism into Aleut and sending it for approval to Russian-speaking translators. By that summer he had despatched a copy to his bishop explaining:

> I had no other object in translating this than that the Aleut who reads or listens to the Catechism in his native language might understand and learn from it what he ought to believe and do for his salvation . . . I dare not assert that the translation is free from insignificant errors – for this is the first work to be composed in . . . a language which has as yet no written grammar; I do however dare assert that with regard to important errors I have neither tolerated through negligence or laziness . . . anything contrary to the Orthodox Faith or Christian law . . . Since many Aleuts can understand Russian, I consider it wise to print it together with the Russian text . . . In my opinion this can be of profound value, inasmuch as those who understand Russian can read the Catechism in Russian, while those who do not can read it in Aleut.[1]

John Veniaminov, who became the first Russian Orthodox bishop to Alaska and the Americas, and is remembered as St Innokent, was a very remarkable man. The first to write down the Aleut language, he also set about producing the first grammar of the language. He translated the liturgy and the Scriptures into the language of the Aleuts, a people exploited and despised by the traders of the Russian–American trading company who nevertheless depended on them for furs. Like other nineteenth-century colonialists, John Veniaminov took it for granted that the Aleut language would not long survive, but in the meantime it had to be studied, used and indeed loved as the means of conveying the gospel to the people he learned to respect and cherish.

Father John and his family lived in the same kind of primitive accommodation as the Aleuts themselves, realizing that the Aleuts knew best how to keep warm, even if smelly, during the long winter. This remarkable missionary and his family lived their faith with simple and passionate devotion. Travelling around by kayak, Veniaminov set up churches, maintained worship, taught the people. Most striking of all, he began to protect the people against the cruelties of the Russian–American Company. The courage and integrity of this Christian family was a most powerful witness for Christianity. Meanwhile Father John kept finding in the native religion signs of the presence of God, which had prepared the way for the gospel – the boundary was already porous.

Eventually Father John – promoted to be Bishop Innokent – became Metropolitan of Moscow and the founder of the Russian Missionary Society, encourager of a vast amount of missionary work of which western Christianity is largely ignorant. He spent, for example, a brief period visiting Japan, and found that the chaplain at the Russian embassy in Tokyo was so depressed by the xenophobic attitudes of the Japanese that he had taken to spending his time reading French novels. Inspired by

Innokent, he began learning Japanese from a traditional Samurai who deeply disapproved of his intention, and then set about translating the liturgy and other texts into Japanese so successfully that the Samurai himself became the first Orthodox priest in Japan and is known in his tradition as Father Nikolai of Tokyo.

Ironically it was the Russian–American fur trading company which had asked the Church in Russia to provide missionaries to Alaska, mainly to meet the needs of the trappers. It was in 1741 that Nicholas Behring had found the route to Alaska through the straits which now bear his name. Following this discovery the great peninsula was opened up for exploitation of its natural resources. In 1793 a group of six monks were sent off to Kodiak Island, one of the Aleutian chain, where they proceeded to preach to and convert the native population. The mission was initially highly successful and the natives extraordinarily receptive to the gospel message. Not surprisingly the imagery of light dawning from on high much appealed to them. The greatest difficulty for the missionaries was to counteract the evidence of the lives and manners of the trappers. The monks were welcomed when it was seen that they would champion the Aleuts against the abuse and contempt of the fur traders who treated them so shamefully. Such championing did not make them popular with the traders; eventually five of the monks either died or returned to Russia. One only remained and went to live the life of a staretz, a characteristically Russian hermit life, on Spruce Island where there is little doubt that his asceticism and gentleness, his capacity to endure as the Aleuts themselves endured, resonated with the spirituality of the native shamans. St Herman lived on in Spruce Island until 1837 when he died at the age of 81.

Herman's mission to his own people, the trading

Russians was probably harder than to the Aleuts. A tale is told of the occasion when he was invited to speak to the ship's officers when a naval vessel anchored at Kodiak Island. He asked them, 'Gentlemen, what do you love more than anything else and what do you wish for your happiness?' Their answers were what you would expect! Wealth, glory, beautiful wives, captaincy of a great vessel. He then asked, 'Is it not true that each of you wishes for what he considers to be the most worthy of love?' They replied, 'Yes, surely.' 'But would you not say that the most worthy of love is our Lord Jesus Christ, who created us, gave life to all creation, nourished us and takes care of us? And shouldn't we love him more than anything else?'

The officers could only agree! Of course they loved God. Everyone had to do that. But Herman rejoined, 'I, a sinner, have been trying for forty years to love God, and I still cannot say that I love him with a perfect love. If we love someone, we always remember that person, try to give him joy, think of him day and night. Do you love God in such a manner, gentlemen? Do you often turn to him? Do you always think of him? Do you always pray to him and fulfil his commandments? Let us,' concluded Herman, 'at least promise to try to love God more than anything else, and to obey his holy will!'

The evidence shows how Russian Orthodox monks acted in their own style and ethos, challenging the worldliness and savage greed of the traders as well as the resistance of the native population whom, with the confidence of nineteenth-century explorers, they cheerfully called 'savages'. Boundaries are not simple constructs. They existed between Russians and Aleuts in both culture and language, between secular Russians (the traders) and the missionaries, between Christianity and the native spiritism of the Aleuts.

In 1841, three years after Herman died, John Veniaminov was sailing by Spruce Island in a great storm and he prayed in intercession to Herman for the storm to cease. The story says that in a quarter of an hour the wind dropped and Veniaminov was saved. Such a direct and simple faith in an intervening God links the Russian not only with the spiritism of the pre-Christian Aleuts, but with the early Celtic saints – more so than with the British missionaries who were in the same period working in the hotter regions of Africa and India.

It would, of course, be foolish to suppose that the conversion of the Aleuts was a simple and unalloyed process. A contemporary Alaskan has remarked that the coming of Christianity to his people was a disaster because the Christians brought division. Even in death he said some are buried as Roman Catholics and some are buried as Protestants and others as Orthodox. Protestantism reached Alaska and the Aleutians because Russia sold them to the USA, which involved the Aleutian people in further difficulties. During the Second World War the islanders were moved from their homes by the Americans, and even now are in the process of trying to get compensation for the destruction of their churches and damage to their early nineteenth-century icons.

The heroism of nineteenth-century mission activity sometimes embarrasses modern Europeans because of its close association with empire and capitalism. The public discourse of the late twentieth century has regarded missionaries as people tainted by their background, cultures and attitudes. Much of that criticism is justified. But embedded in that ambivalent history there are stories of a purity of vision, a love of humanity and a detachment from the standards of the missionaries' own world-background that glow. Crossing continents to make converts was a commitment to remaining in poverty, facing discouragement and failure. Yet many of them left in the memories of the people an image of goodness and vulnerable love which conveyed something of their vision of God. There are in the tales of the missionaries stories of communication across barriers of language and culture which made new beginnings possible.

The title or caption on the cross of Christ proclaimed in three languages – Hebrew, Latin and Greek – that here was 'the King of the Jews'. So the language of the Roman empire, the language of the cultured Greek world resented by many Romans, and the Semitic language of Jesus' origin, were all part of the world in which Jesus lived. The story of Pentecost itself portrays the coming of the Holy Spirit as a gift, which reunites humanity, a new humanity in Christ. The truth is proclaimed in a way in which all the languages of the earth may understand. Interpreted in this way the Pentecost event as portrayed in the book of Acts is seen as a reversal of the judgement of Babel. There the skills of humanity are seen as aspiring to threaten God, and God's judgement was understood to have brought down a curse of language division as a punishment, and as a means of preventing such overweening pride ever again. The undoubted usefulness of a lingua franca has tended to sustain the idea of many languages as a curse rather than as a blessing. But it is equally possible theologically to interpret the many languages of the world as God's way of preventing one people or one language from gaining the upper hand. The gift of the Holy Spirit then enables peoples, despite their linguistic divisions, to be united in understanding of the message of the gospel.

The linguistic groups represented on the title on the cross represent in a sense the three great divisions within the worldwide church: the Oriental churches, the Greek-speaking churches with their Slavonic derivatives, and the Latin West. Although Greek was the common language of most of the earliest Christians, linguistic separation was inevitable as the faith spread. Latin became a major theological language alongside Greek in the West, while the Syrian and Coptic churches used their own tongues. Latin and Greek were each of them valid as a lingua franca within widespread élites, and the sacred texts and liturgies were long given protected status which was at odds with the need to evangelize in languages understood by the people. Nevertheless, the Christian faith helped preserve the lingua franca status of the two languages while linguistic change went on in the secular world. This meant the promotion of literacy, at least within a privileged clerical class, and the maintenance of cultures, which crossed over tribal boundaries.

When beyond Europe Christianity has come into cultures on the coat-tails of empire, the need of secular power to ensure submission sometimes came into conflict with the need of the Church to convey its message in a way in which it can be heard in a new community and culture. The languages of empires have thus been vehicles for carrying the gospel, while the gift of the Holy Spirit is needed to give hearts to preachers to love their converts, and ears to converts to hear and respond to the new. Over and over again the dual process of proclaiming the gospel and imposing stable governance has produced an ambiguity of purpose.

Within Europe itself the build-up of pressure to translate the Scriptures into the vernacular languages in the fifteenth century was caused partly by the invention of printing, partly by Martin Luther's challenge on behalf of the vulgar tongues, partly by the challenge of nation-states to the pope. When in 1563 Elizabeth I's government passed an act of parliament for the translation of the Bible into Welsh (only finally accomplished in 1588), the need to preserve the unity of her Protestant kingdom was at least as important as the need to save souls. The government feared that a recusant Wales would return to its former rebellious state. The language boundary could not be allowed to prejudice the security of the state's territorial boundaries; a disaffected Wales would have offered an easy landing-point for Catholic invaders. Again we see the complexity of boundaries – between Welsh and English, between the imperial and the subject people (who in this case had accepted their status in good part), between Catholic and Protestant, between the imperial powers themselves.

However, there is in Europe an earlier European model for the use of a 'local' language – the mission of Cyril and Methodius, who in the ninth century set off from Constantinople to reform the Church in Moravia – the modern Czech Republic and Slovakia. Previous Frankish missionaries had imposed a Latin system on the people, but Cyril created an alphabet for the Slavonic languages, which still bears his name, Cyrillic. He set about translating the Scriptures and other liturgical texts in what we now call Church or Old Slavonic. Methodius completed the translation of the Bible before he died in 885. Their wise and truly eirenic way of gospel proclamation was different from the imperial methods of the Frankish missionaries. (It is of course ironic that Church Slavonic eventually became a sacred language with a similar status to Latin in medieval Europe.)

Since those missionary times linguistic and theological divisions in the Balkans developed along the fault lines between church structures and theologies, with the additional complication of the spread of Islam. Ethnic differences are reinforced by language, theology, culture and power – both imperial and ecclesiastical. We might find at one level a rich and varied response to gospel, but also testimony to the capacity of human pride to miss the point of the gospel and to refuse the gift of understanding the voice of God in different languages.

If the coming of the gospel to a people is experienced as new hope then it begins many complex processes in the receiving society. But it is inevitably compromised when accompanied by military or mercantile enforcement. The gospel story of Jesus has to be told and the meaning of it conveyed. In this the telling of the story, the translation of Scriptures and the provision of liturgies into different languages has been vital. Frequently clashes with state or military power have led to the witness of martyrdom. So often one has a sense of waste and failure resulting from such conflicts between gospel and culture or between gospel and power.

When the gospel came with conquest, as for example in the case of Charlemagne, there was a demand for cultural surrender. The ancient Saxon Easter liturgy contained this passage:

Do you forsake the devil?
I forsake the devil.
And the guild of devils?
I forsake the whole guild of devils.
And all the works of the devil?
and I forsake all the works and words of the devil,
Donar and Wodan and Saxnot
and all the evil spirits who are their allies.[2]

Such capitulation was as much a political issue as a religious one. In the main the Germanic gods were state gods, and so the new rulers needed to make it plain that the new Christian God was more powerful. The nature of God's power and the way in which God might choose to use it or not use it is immensely important to the integrity of the faith, though in different periods it has been distorted in different ways. The wielders of worldly power have always been ready to use the faith (and not only the Christian faith) as a vehicle for their own political and mercantile power, whether ninth-century European emperors, twelfth-century Normans, eighteenth-century Russians, or English, Portuguese and Spanish slave traders.

The process of crossing the boundary of faith-culture has usually involved bringing the stories and myths of the native culture into the light of the gospel and reinterpreting them. Because of the importance of the written word in Christianity, the way in which the Bible and the language of worship hold the meaning of the faith, the coming of the gospel often began the process of change from an oral/aural culture to a written culture – one of human civilization's greatest cultural boundaries. The boundary survives in literary evidence. We can see in the medieval literatures of Europe a process of first or second-generation Christians telling the stories of their pre-Christian ancestors, splendidly exemplified in the Anglo-Saxon epic, *Beowulf*. Even many generations later Christian writers were aware that there had been other times, other customs: in the early Welsh tale *Pwyll, Pendefig Dyfed* there is reference to the birth of a child and the fact that he was baptized 'with the baptism they had in that time'.

Just as those and other writers showed awareness of the pagan–Christian interface, so Christian stories could be adapted to the culture in which they were related. In the ninth century a Christian Saxon told the story of Christ in a poem called the Heliand (the Saviour). The detail of the story is Germanic. The ships on the Sea of Galilee turn into high-prowed northern vessels, and the disciples are a band of heroes enraged by the soldiers who come to arrest Jesus. Jesus himself is a heroic prince-figure who sounds not at all like modern versions of him. Even the pagan gods had been under the power of Wyrd (Fate), but the hope of the gospel, which the poem conveys is that Christ overcomes the power of Fate. The trappings and detail become Germanized, but the heart-message of the poem is the defeat of the Germanic concept of inscrutable Fate. Similarly in the lovely Old English poem *The Dream of the Rood* (rood = cross) Jesus is presented as a hero who climbs up onto the cross not in humiliation but in triumph. From this distance we can see the boundary, the ragged seam where two pieces of cloth come together. We recognize the epic northern society fastening onto the elements in the Gospel story which seem to them most compatible and accessible to their own culture.

Bible Study

Jesus' first sermon in Nazareth
Luke 4.14b–30

St Luke's account of the birth of Jesus and the events of his childhood contain the essence of the gospel in symbolic form. The weaving of story and canticle with references to the Old Testament conjures up the world of the early Jewish Christian community and the way in which they understood the gospel message. In the account of Jesus' first sermon in Nazareth there is an account in miniature of his whole ministry.[3] Luke frequently puts in his writing fore-tastes of what will come later, and the account of the temptations in the wilderness lays out the themes that will emerge, re-emerge and come to full fruition in the passion narrative. In this account in chapter 4 of Jesus' appearance in the synagogue at Nazareth we find him welcomed and listened to with great attention and delight. His reputation as a teacher in Galilee has gone before him, but soon questions are raised about who he is; doubts are expressed and things turn sour. By reading the passage from Isaiah he proclaims the nature of his ministry and the doubts grow, turning into rage and violent rejection. That pattern in Nazareth prefigures what happens during the ministry of Jesus, leading up to the passion and crucifixion in Jerusalem. But it is a difficult passage, condensed and allusive, and it is not immediately clear what precipitates this early rejection in his home town. Because there is so much important material in the section there is much disagreement about its significance.

The drama begins in the framework of a service in the synagogue, and all happens so quickly that it is difficult at first to see what triggers the process of rejection and attempted lynching. The evangelist writes so tightly, with so little explanation, that it demands some untangling. This is the running order presented to us:

Jesus goes to the synagogue and stands up to read.

- He reads the passage from Isaiah 61.
- He pronounces that the prophecy has been fulfilled.
- There is a response of welcome and delight.
- They question who he is – he is merely 'Joseph's son'.
- The atmosphere changes because there are no miracles.
- Jesus speaks of healings of foreigners by the prophets.
- There is great anger and they try to lynch him.
- He goes on his way.

The change of atmosphere happens within verse 22. Luke

may be combining two stories or episodes and the seam shows, although there is no link passage or indication of whether any time has passed between the warm response and the beginning of the questioning and the expression of doubt. But the evangelist indicates that the people of Nazareth (and so eventually the people of Jerusalem and Israel) are worried about who he is, and they want to see more miracles for themselves. The hunger for miracles brings crowds who frequently make things difficult for Jesus and the disciples. The uncertainty and questioning boil over into rage when Jesus brings up the issue of healings of foreigners by the prophets. Why does the subject arise? Why should that have been so infuriating? It has to do with the relationship of Israel to the nations, and is a pointer to the interpretation of Jesus as saviour for the whole world, not only Israel. The book of the Acts of the Apostles will begin with an account of the nations coming to Jerusalem and understanding each other. Here the ministry of Jesus begins with a violent rejection among Jesus' own people.

The key to the unease must be in the text that he chooses to read. The verses are from the beginning of Isaiah 61, which are just the opening of a longer section. Did Jesus actually read the whole passage, while Luke merely indicates the opening verses, or was he being very precise about where Jesus closed the reading? Or does breaking off the reading at that point show Luke's interpretation of the reason for the rejection of Jesus in his own home town? There are passages in Scripture that people know by heart; those who read Scripture in church know that the quality of the listening is different when people are echoing the words themselves in their memories. It may be fanciful to suggest that the people in the synagogue in Nazareth were listening like that – intensely and closely, and perhaps waiting for the 'next bit' – which doesn't come. Jesus sits down in a still-expectant silence, having announced:

> The Spirit of the Lord is upon me, because he has anointed me to bring good news to the poor. He has sent me to proclaim release to the prisoners and recovery of sight to the blind, to let the oppressed go free, to proclaim the year of the Lord's favour. (Luke 4.18–19)

It is hard to see why such a reading on its own would evoke hostility – and at first it does not. Jesus rolls the scroll up and says that the prophecy has come true among them. But something in that reading and interpretation of Isaiah in Nazareth must have set alarm bells ringing and started a discussion which is indicated only minimally in the rest of the narrative. What was so infuriating that they should have tried to lynch him?

Luke briefly indicates what follows when Jesus gives examples from the Hebrew Scriptures of God's gracious acts through the prophets to people beyond the boundaries of Israel. He quotes two examples. First the healing by the prophet Elijah of the widow's son in Zarephath in Sidon (1 Kings 7.7–24). Why should Elijah have squandered his generosity on such a person? The work of the prophets – and of God therefore – was not confined to the people of Israel. Jesus asks whether there were not enough needy people and widows in Israel in Elijah's time? He then gives a second example – Naaman the Syrian general who overcame the King of Israel (2 Kings 5). Were there not enough lepers in Israel for him to heal, asks Jesus ironically. The argument seems to be that on this evidence God has wider things in store, and that the Jews are not the only people in whom God is interested. Moreover, the healing of Naaman indicates the lack of faith among the leadership of the people at that time.

> When they heard this, all in the synagogue were filled with rage. They got up, drove him out of the town and led him to the brow of the hill on which their town was built, so that they might hurl him off the cliff. But he passed through the midst of them and went on his way. (Luke 4.28–30)

But it is not only the direct references to these two events that enrage the crowd. There is another clue to the change of mood in what is not said, in the words of Scripture that Jesus omits. He sits down in mid-sentence, and the quotation from Isaiah 'to proclaim the year of the Lord's favour' breaks off before 'the day of vengeance of our God' which is the climax of the sentence.

We know very well how the human longing for justice readily spills over into a desire for revenge. The expectation of God's vengeance was the hope to which the disciples on the road to Emmaus were still clinging after the resurrection. They tell the unrecognized Jesus going along with them: 'We had hoped that he was the one who would redeem Israel.' Vindication of ourselves against those who have humiliated us is instinctive in us. It is the deep longing of every oppressed group that eventually the oppressor will not only be thrown off but will be punished. It is a sentiment expressed eloquently in the psalms. This was a people much trampled upon, a people longing for God to do something, to restore the kingdom to Israel.

There are two ways of reading the episode. If you want to read it in a 'this is what happened in Nazareth on that occasion' way, then you could perhaps ask, 'Did Jesus know the politics of his congregation?' Did he know individuals in the crowd who were so convinced of the rightness of their cause that they would not even consider for a moment that God might give a thought to the nations around them. The passage quoted by Jesus goes on to describe eloquently the victory and justification of the suffering and humiliated people of God. But Jesus leaves out the appeal for vengeance and even the delight in triumph. Modern ears may not notice the gap, but the omission of what in fact is the climax of the reading, a climax enlarged upon in following sections, must have been a strong statement. The echoing absence of the crucial phrase would have struck a congregation that knew their Scriptures better than we do, and it would have dawned on them that here was an acute critique of their victim culture and of their longing for vengeance.

The congregation's culture is radically challenged – by one of their own. It is the culture of the oppressed group, the oppressed nation convinced of its own calling by God, convinced of its own suffering and justified by its loyalty to the covenant. What? No day of vengeance? A new light is being cast by Jesus himself on the doctrine of the special chosen-ness of Israel, its election by God. The people of Nazareth do what the Pharisees would do later, what the people of Israel formerly did to the prophets, which was to try to silence Jesus. He had thrown down a gauntlet to his community and they had recognized the challenge. Is it then that Jesus is challenging his people, right at the beginning of his ministry, to abandon their longing for vengeance? Is it that his meditation in the desert has brought him to the conclusion that the Spirit of God is not compatible with such longing? If that is so, then the prayer of Jesus at the crucifixion for forgiveness for the Jews and the Romans is a poignant echo of this initial rejection and near lynching in Nazareth.

Though the passage may be interpreted as if it were an episode, it must surely also be read as a profound theological statement by Luke. Just as in the infancy narrative he contains his message of salvation in miniature, so in this early episode in the ministry of Jesus a theme is introduced which will be replayed and elaborated throughout the Gospel. In the Hebrew Scriptures there is a self-under-standing of the nation as being chosen by God, ruled by a divinely chosen royal dynasty, worshipping in a centralized cult in the temple, keeping the law in great detail, and keep-ing itself apart from other nations. However, there is with-in the Hebrew Scriptures a contradictory argument: the book of Ruth argues against the story of Nehemiah, show-ing what riches come to the nation through outsiders. Matthew highlights this thread in his genealogy of Joseph. This universalist theme, in which the people of God are to be the light to the nations, is particularly strong in Isaiah. The interpretation presented by Jesus so soon after his preparation for ministry in the desert is so sharp and threatening that at the very beginning of his ministry his life is threatened. In this overture, as it were, Luke is showing how it will all end.

So what does all this say to oppressed and oppressing structures today? It certainly shows how difficult it is to expect victims to acknowledge their part in the situation. It shows how the crowd in Nazareth were unable to hear what Jesus was telling them even when he did so simply by leaving out a phrase that they wanted to hear – 'the day of vengeance of our God'. Their own expectation was so clearly defined that suggesting that others – outsiders – may be instruments of God's purpose or recipients of God's grace was grossly offensive.

Yet how can the call for justice work except in a culture of forgiveness? The voice which excludes vengeance from the agenda of the peoples is the voice that needs to be heard in every area of the world where old hatreds and unforgivingness are nurtured and fed. In South Africa the

Commission of Justice and Reconciliation chaired by Bishop Desmond Tutu illustrates the depth of forgiveness demanded in order to make it possible for people to move on into a better future. There were people – particularly commentators from Europe who had foretold a blood bath, who felt that the measure of forgiveness asked was intolerable. To tell the wounded not to seek their own vengeance – on the West Bank, in Srebreniça, in Mostva, in Belfast, in the Indian reservations of North America, at Ground Zero, in Rwanda, in Iraq, sounds like allowing the powers of darkness to get away with their wickedness. What is even more difficult is expecting oppressors to forgive those who dare protest.

Luke's particular preoccupation is with the bringing of the gospel to the gentiles. He shows Jesus at the very beginning of his ministry raising the issue of whether God has favourites. Is this new faith coming from this little people on the turbulent eastern edge of the Roman empire big enough for the Romans? Is this God big enough to replace the state gods of Rome? Here Jesus indicates a path, which brings him into conflict with the high priest and Pilate, with his own people and his people's most recent conquerors. It is the political world of resentment and fear, of the rage of the oppressed and the contempt of the powerful, which we recognize from the conflicts of our own day. The theme set out by Luke is that the power of vulnerable forgiveness and trust is going to transform things. The difficulty, the scandal and stumbling block of the message to angry and hurt people is seen through the whole history of the Church. Time and again people fail to live by what Jesus offers. But again and again there are examples of those whose love and forgiveness have transformed their communities.

Within the New Testament there is an extraordinary

example of a 'more excellent way', in which Paul struggles with the issue of slavery. The power of the Roman empire was built on slavery. Any attempt to shake it by political means was doomed to failure, and the fact that so many slaves and women came into the early Christian Church, finding new dignity and value, presented the leaders with considerable difficulty. A world without slavery must have seemed unimaginable. For the Jews, whose experience of slavery in Egypt was a basic, self-defining experience, the structure of the Roman system was particularly offensive. It is significant that Paul uses the imagery of slavery and remission, of buying freedom, of the yoke of slavery, to explain how the salvation of Jesus works.

The imperative of the gospel was to override slavery completely, yet the economic and political structure of the early Church and its littleness and vulnerability could not begin to argue such a case. Paul's caution suggests that there were some who wanted to do just that. The Church brought imperial rage down on itself soon enough without needing to encourage a revolt of slaves as well. The letter to Philemon shows how Paul dealt with the situation in a practical way, though it is a way which does not appeal to modern readers. Paul writes from prison in Rome to a friend at Colossae called Philemon. A slave owned by Philemon called Onesimus (which means 'of value to' or 'profitable') has run away from his owner and taken money with him. Since coming to Rome he has become a Christian and has been valuable and profitable to Paul. Paul writes to Philemon who as the owner of the slave could perfectly well insist on his right of punishment, even by death, for his run-away slave, and sends Onesimus to carry this letter commending the slave as a Christian to his Christian owner. Paul is asking both of them to establish a relationship in Christ that accepts what the secular law says, but he expects that relationship to transcend that law and be rooted in mutual forgiveness, vulnerability and trust. Given that slavery exists, then individuals caught in the trap of that relationship might point to a transformed relationship. Paul does not write encouraging Onesimus or Philemon to work for the overthrowal of slavery as an institution, any more than he could encourage women to reject their subordinate status within secular society. The boundary cannot be abolished, but it can be bridged by love.

Paul's letter to Philemon, the Christian slave-owner, is an extraordinary example of promoting a transformed relationship within an evil structure. In any case it is not entirely clear that Paul, being a man of his own time, regarded slavery as evil in itself; it was a feature of human society and a basic fact of life. Rather Paul perceives it as something that ought to be irrelevant if people are related to each other in Christ. Paul treats both Onesimus and Philemon with great dignity, pleading at once for Philemon to abandon his legal rights over Onesimus, while persuading Onesimus by taking the letter to Philemon to acknowledge that in the world of the flesh this man has power of ownership, indeed of life or death over him. A culture without slavery could not be imagined although it is indicated in the letter to the Galatians: 'There is no longer Jew or Greek, there is no longer slave or free, there is no longer male and female; for all of you are one in Christ Jesus' (Gal. 3.28). The problem then is how are Christians to live as free in a society, which accepts slavery and subordinates women.

No doubt that same reasoning is behind the argument in Paul's letter to the Romans discouraging radical thinking in the Christian community. Again there is a kind of acceptance that the world cannot be changed, but that Christians can transform their own world by living according to the standards of the kingdom of heaven – leading eventually to Augustine's idea of the two cities, the earthly city and the heavenly city.

The American New Testament scholar Walter Wink suggests that in our current world of international capitalism – which we cannot overthrow – we should simply recognize it as The System, in whose earthly city we have to live, but we ourselves as Christians should live according to an entirely different standard. In the same way the yeast which is put into the flour has the potential to transform the whole of it. As we have seen, Paul's appeal to the Philippians uses the image of resident aliens or sojourners, a status, which ought to suffice for us. The truth, however, is that we want to move from tents into palaces, making our situation permanent and stable. Paul's idea is that of being among the cultures and nations of the world and yet not belonging. It is therefore not appropriate for any people to call themselves a Christian nation. Christian nations, so-called, have attacked each other and nations recognizing other faiths, and continue to do so.

When Paul writes to Philemon asking him to abandon his legal rights as a citizen over his slave property, it is Christ's challenge to the economy of the Roman empire and an undermining of the structure of the state. When young Roman girls took to refusing marriage in order to be devoted to Christ, it was not so much an unhealthy fear of their sexuality that enraged their families as the realization that for young girls to disobey their fathers and refuse to be mothers would totally undermine the social structure as they understood it. For young women to choose a life not determined by the needs of society and the state was as dangerous as challenging slavery. Within the Church, centuries later, women's orders were kept firmly under the control of the male religious orders and the most brilliant women like Hildegard of Bingen wrote of themselves, in the sad phrase, as being 'only women'. The struggle within the Anglican Church in the last 50 years over the ordination of women to the priesthood has shown how the culture and assumptions of the Roman world, petrified within the Church, reveals a theology which contradicts the revolutionary good news that in Christ there is neither male nor female.

Cultures have a way of mutating to accommodate challenges rather than meet them, and the Church itself takes on characteristics of the society in which it lives and can be as hidebound by cultural assumptions as that society. The great danger is that after initially challenging a culture, Christians settle down to make the most of it. There leaps to mind the image of St Augustine abandoning the mother of his child in order to organize a marriage with a wealthier woman, which he does not go through with.

It seems fairer to assume that the gospel ought to be always challenging a culture. When a culture claims to be Christian by definition, alarm bells should ring. We may consider for example the culture of Poland. It is deeply Catholic and the Church has generated a culture rich in images of the gospel. Early twentieth-century Welsh Nonconformists made similar claims for Welsh society. The United States (despite the separation of church and state) regards itself as sustaining Christian values. But the danger is that a culture changed by the gospel and then shaped by the Church in a particular form is not necessarily true to the gospel. The culture itself will quickly dislodge the figure of Christ. We ourselves become our own idols; what we have achieved, what we love, is what has to be defended against other cultures. It emerges in different forms according to whether the nation concerned is an assertive and empire-building one, or whether it is a weak, vulnerable one that like Israel perceives itself to be the victim of others. At best both cultures are semi-Christian.

We may consider, for example, the speed with which war fever spread through Britain at the beginning of the First World War. Think how Christian leaders led the campaigns for volunteers. Welsh Presbyterian ministers did it with as much enthusiasm as English and Welsh bishops. Christian communities gave those who opposed the war a tough time. The boundaries between nations are deeply incised with every war, with every battle, with every act of domination.

Questions

1 What is your instinctive, gut reaction when you hear a different language spoken. Does it alienate or intrigue you? Why?

2 Is there an aspect of the culture of the Christian group or church to which you belong which makes you feel uncomfortable?

3 If you were sent to live in a totally different culture, Japan or China, or a tribal reservation in Brazil, what in your own Christian culture would you be most grieved to lose?

4 In what way would you seek to replace what you missed?

5 How would you explain your actions to your neighbours in your new environment?

6

Between Public and Personal: The Lament of History

The young chief was caught in a dilemma. As leader of his people it was immensely important for him to have a son. His much-loved wife had had four babies, but each one had died; the death of one child after another had became not just a personal tragedy but a danger hanging over the people. Patriarchal and polygamous, the tribe required of its chief that he should father a son. Reluctantly, looking to the needs and traditions of his people, he took a second wife. His first beloved and bereaved wife submitted to the inevitable. It was the pattern of the old world from which they came; they realized that there could not be for them the new pattern of marriage proffered by the Christian missionaries. The old culture's polygamy was significant at many levels. It was unacceptable for a woman not to be married, but there were always more women than men. A plurality of wives was associated with wealth and prestige, and in a society which had accepted polygamy without question it was easier for women to work together for mutual support, ensuring that men accepted their protective responsibility. Polygamy did not preclude a level of female independence and subversiveness. Above all, it rendered more likely the birth and survival of an heir. It is hardly surprising that the people found the Christian doctrine of marriage difficult. They were torn between the security and practicality of the old and the challenge and danger of the new.

The chief's decision, supported by his people, that he should take a second wife, was a huge disappointment to the missionary who had come to the tribe. The young chief and his wife had been listening to his teaching and seemed ready to take the next step of being baptized. But it was out of the question for a Christian missionary to baptize a man who had more than one wife. So, no doubt regretfully, the door into the Christian faith was shut. However, the acquiring of a second wife did not solve the problem of a male heir, for again it was a case of hope followed by grief. The second wife had two babies, a boy who died, followed by a disappointing girl. The grieving and desperate chief took a third wife who had a daughter who died, then a miscarriage.

But in the meantime and against the odds, the first wife had a child, a boy who lived, and was given the name Abilete, meaning 'The Lord has blessed me in the birth of a son'. The chief and his three wives remained on the fringe of the growing Christian community, for there was a real problem about their relationship to the Church. Despite their faith-response to the message of salvation in Christ, they had submitted to the requirements of the tribal culture. The chief had fulfilled his responsibilities and had taken on two additional wives because of his duty as a chief to provide a male heir. The European missionary was adamant, standing true to his understanding of the faith, that a man with more than one wife could not be baptized a Christian unless he renounced all but the first. But for the chief, there was an acute moral problem, not only of who would look after his cast-off wives, but what would happen to other cast-off wives – not to mention their children – if the men in the tribe were to imitate their chief? A change of religious allegiance would be dangerous and painful at both a public and a personal level.

The first wife's situation was poignant indeed. She could have been baptized, since her position, from the point of view of the missionary, was of the 'true' wife. No concubine she – it was not her fault, and she was not responsible for the existence of the other two wives. But she refused to be 'separated' from her husband by baptism because, she said, she would not choose to enter heaven if her husband did not enter too. There on the boundary between such different cultures we glimpse the cross taken up by that African family. The story illustrates vividly the pain of change for a people on the border between two cultures and two faiths. It was also a boundary between the personal and the public, between individual and community needs. Those boundaries were truly painful.

There is an ironic sequel to the story. The boy was brought up in the new faith, and when old enough to affirm his personal faith he prepared to be baptized. The custom, indeed the expectation, was for converts to abandon their African names and take biblical and western names. But the young man, while taking on the additional biblical name, refused to abandon his given African name, Abilete, the name that told his story and the story of his family and tribe, 'The Lord has blessed me in the birth of a son'.

This poignant story was told to me by Abilete himself, smiling gently as he did so, regretful but not angry as he told the story of his people's journey into the faith of Christ, of which he himself is a minister. He told me his story in the city of Salvador in Bahia, in Brazil. The city at that time (December 1996) was just beginning to reap the fruits of investment in new hotels and the refurbishment of its colonial architecture as sightseeing attractions for tourists. The old Portuguese houses in the centre of the city were being repaired and repainted in delicious sugared-almond colours. New roads had been carved along the coast, linking skyscraper air-conditioned hotels to the airport. It was in one of these hotels that, inappropriately but inevitably, the delegates to the conference were based. The Council for World Mission and Evangelism had organized coaches to take the delegates down to the old port of Salvador, where for centuries slaves had been disgorged from the holds of ships from West Africa.

Salvador was the original colonial capital of the country carved out on the Portuguese maps as Brazil. In 1550 the Portuguese who colonized that huge tract of South America were among the first to import West African slaves to do the work of harvesting sugar, work that they could neither persuade nor coerce the natives of the area to do. The slave ships brought Africans over from what is now Ghana, where they had been kept for a time in a slave fort on the Cape Coast. They were kept there long enough to fill a ship, and because they had lost so much weight in the fort there was all the more room to cram the ships. The result was heavy loss of life on the journey over to South America. Those who survived were unloaded onto the quayside at Solar Do Unhao and classified according to size, age, gender, and state of health. They were kept in underground dungeons until they were brought out and marched up to stand in front of a church that had been built nearby. There, buckets of water were poured over them, not so much to wash them, as to be able to say in the slave-market that these were baptized slaves. Baptized slaves were deemed more tractable and less volatile, and therefore they sold for a better price. For baptized read 'value added'.

In 1996 the several hundred members of the conference were taken down to the quayside for a service of reconciliation. West African Christians gave to Brazilian descendants of those early slaves a stone brought from the castle on the coast of Ghana. Twentieth-century Christians from all over the world went through a ritual of repentance, forgiveness and renewal, based on a rite developed in post-apartheid South Africa under the guidance of Archbishop Desmond Tutu. They took water in their hands from common bowls and washed their faces together. They put on little cotton friendship bands and tied them for each other.

Salvador was a city built on slavery. The old Portuguese colonial part of the city, known as Pelhourino, used to be where the slave-owners lived. Some time in the eighteenth century bubonic plague swept through the city, so the rich all moved out to seek safety beyond the city limits. The poor took over the houses abandoned by their owners and lived in that area until very recently. Then the government realized that in the old Pelhourino area there was a 'heritage' resource with great potential for international tourism. But the place would need to be smartened up – so of course the poor were moved on.

The name Pelhourino is significant. When slavery was at its height there stood at the centre of the square a huge pillar called a belhor. Runaway or troublesome slaves would be tied to the belhor and scourged. It was both punishment and warning. In the nineteenth century when the campaign to abolish slavery gained strength, pressure was brought on the government to abolish this method of discipline. Reluctantly the old belhor was taken down and a smaller one, a belhourino, put in its place. The belhourino, the little whipping post in the place of punishment and tyranny, has become the new playground of the international tourist. Bars and souvenir shops now surround the square, which ran with the blood of slaves, for tourists, from whom the descendants of the slaves, with huge smiles and pounding drums, cheerfully take their dollars.

The two churches built by the slave-owners in Belhourino are a terrible reproach to those who cling to the ideal of Christian European civilization. The dedications seem ironic to us today – one is dedicated to St Francis Xavier, the pioneer missionary, the other to St Francis of Assisi, the saint of poverty. The interiors of both churches are covered in gold. In one a set of pillars meant to represent the columns of Solomon's temple show the orders of society in order descending from the top: kings, priests, soldiers, scholars. At the bottom of the columns, holding them up, are the slaves. Perhaps King Solomon with his forced labourers building the temple would not have thought it odd. Thus did the descendants of the counter-Reformation signal their triumph in South America, interpreting their culture even as they distorted the gospel. Church buildings sometimes reflect secular culture more vividly than the God who is ostensibly worshipped in them. It might be fruitful to consider Westminster Abbey or St Paul's Cathedral, many a parish church and not a few chapels in that light.

The story of the Christian faith in South America is thus distorted by the empire that surrounded the Church. But we do not have to go as far as South America to be aware of another scar on the face of Christendom, one consistently pointed to as evidence of the evil influence of all religion. In Northern Ireland Protestant and Catholic Christian cultures inheriting so much poison from the past, have been caught up in commitment to murder and revenge.

Imagine then a group of three teenage boys brought up in the heart of the Protestant community. Their great-grand-fathers had been involved in the Carson-led resistance to home rule in Ireland. They were founders of Orange Order lodges; they marched in the summer to remember King

Billy. Family, street tradition and identity were all deeply involved. They loved the bands, the whistles and the songs. Their fathers and uncles wore the orange sashes and the bowler hats that are the tribal vestments of Protestant supremacy in the North.

The three lads had planned an evening out together. But one backed out. He had persuaded a girl to go out with him. It was his first date. The other two may have been envious. They went off together and that night met some other lads who talked to them about doing something to protect their community against the Catholics. They became involved with a paramilitary group. Some years later, as a result of that encounter, one of them was shot and the other had his kneecaps shot through. The third lad, who at that time shared the same background and attitudes as his boyhood companions, thanks to a childhood sweetheart, was free to take another path.

That boy, became a Methodist minister passionately committed, not to defending the Protestant cause and the Orange Order, but to rebuilding community in peace. The church to which he is minister is on the so-called peace line in Belfast, using every means available to provide safe space and quality accommodation, while building bridges to the Catholics on the other side of the road. To choose such a path in Ireland means being literally, as well as metaphorically, on the boundaries, being vulnerable not only to reproach but to reprisal for betraying principles, roots and culture – for being 'Judas' to us the Protestants.

When the secular press accuses Christianity of being the cause of the difficulties in Ireland, Christians sometimes try to deny it, arguing that the issues have to do with colonization and oppression, with power and class issues; religion is just the identifying badge of tribal loyalties. There is an element of truth in that. But Gary Mason[1] seeks to persuade the Christian community to face and understand its own responsibility, its need for repentance, by facing theological issues that have made the churches, both Protestant and Catholic complicit in the murderous conflict, so feebly called 'the Troubles'. There are, he suggests, three theological dogmas which have helped define and petrify divisions and which are used by both sides to support their tribal identities and histories.

The first and ancient dogma is that there is 'no salvation outside the Church'; this powered the early missionary passion of the Church. If you offer salvation, then logically a warning hangs over those who refuse it. It produces the understanding of the Church as an ark, like Noah's, and naturally those outside drown. But when Christianity was persecuted by the state it produced division in the Christian community. St Augustine in the fifth century led the Catholic wing in a bitter argument with the group called Donatists who argued that only those who had resisted the state to martyrdom could be truly Church. The Donatists refused to receive back into communion those bishops who had for a time capitulated or compromised with the powers of the empire. They were confronted and persecuted by the Catholic wing, who argued that such absolutism was unacceptable.

The Roman Catholic Church sustained the dogma of 'no salvation outside The Church' over the centuries with great vigour; in Northern Ireland, ironically, its essence is also sustained by Presbyterians, who believe that those not of their theology and experience are damned. Presbyterians in Northern Ireland will not belong to the ecumenical instrument of Churches Together in Britain and Ireland (CTBI) because Roman Catholics are involved. Many of the new evangelical house churches, the traditional Pentecostal movements and Restoration churches refuse to be involved in relationships with other churches for the same reason. Within different denominations there are conservatives who perceive their role to be maintaining the purity of the faith usually by excluding others. Within Anglicanism 'Reform' seeks to exclude women and homosexuals from the clergy and believes that anyone not with them is against them.

The second dogma highlighted by Gary Mason derives from the first and goes back to St Augustine and his argument with the Donatists. This declares that 'error has no rights'. If your theology, in our judgement is wrong, if your ideas of the Church, of Christ, of Scripture are different from ours then we, who are correct, have the right to trample over you, to deprive you of your civic as well as your religious freedom. Thus the Orthodox Church in post-Soviet Russia persecutes not only invasive evangelical sects from America, but native Baptists as well, their own dissident believers. Instead of allowing the truth that you think you have to speak for itself, the truth is defended by attacking others and using the power of state, police and army to enforce that truth. It is an avoidance of the way of the cross.

Lastly, and logically enough, there is the doctrine of providence. If we are right then God must be on our side. According to the political situation in which the Church finds itself, this produces different cultures. Thus the doctrine of providence produces in the United States a culture of believing that the country is 'one nation under God', which is called by God to set an example to the world, impressing its world-view on others by propaganda, by trade and sometimes by force. In this respect it is the inheritor of the British empire, which itself arose in part from its conflict with the Catholic Spanish empire, which believed itself to be the natural ruler, empowered by the pope and therefore by God, of the New World.

It is, of course, true that even cultures sharing the same

faith may differ widely. The cultures of Catholic Spain and Catholic Ireland are different partly because the political situation of these nations has always been very different. The Protestant culture of Northern Ireland, although dominant in its environment for centuries, perceives itself as an embattled outpost, a remnant faithful to the crown, threatened from within and without, while English Protestant culture has only had to cope with the threat of foreign powers. It is not easy for people within cultures to submit to a challenging critique of axioms, their fundamental assumptions. You may fall short of what I believe to be gospel values – but can you seriously suggest that I, too, am wanting? Those who are powerful find it humiliating, while those who are besieged minorities feel it threatens their very existence.

When the divide is between different faiths then the scene is set for the present menacing clash between radical Islam rooted in resentment of western imperialism and the United States of America. There, 'one nation under God' has inherited in a mutated form the dogmas that nurture violence in a Christian context. Al Quaida too seeks to drive out and destroy the infidel imperialist. Religion is used to reinforce the human instinct to drive out what is perceived as threat.

The words of the African theologian, Dr Musimbi Kanyoro, sum up the pain of recognizing our own complicity in violence when she asks, 'Who shall release us from the lament of history?'[2] For in Africa as in Ireland, as in the Balkans, Christians have been sucked into tribal, cultural and economic wars and lent the power of Christian identity to secular powers to support their cause. Dr Kanyoro spoke vividly for African women and from her experience attempted to find a gospel standpoint between cultures and ecclesial systems, between states and churches.

Neither gospel nor culture is good news until it liberates. There is no gospel or culture that is automatically liberating.

Because the gospel went to Africa accompanied by so much European cultural baggage, it was inevitable that Africa should respond by glorifying its own culture. Dr Kanyoro's challenge was for us 'to work creatively with cultures and traditions so that they can be liberating'. If cultural values rule supreme we risk tolerating much injustice, not least to women, because traditional cultures and religions have frequently cramped and imprisoned women. To tolerate genital mutilation of girls is a grotesque tradition. But conservative Christian theology too has connived with cultural patterns to infantilize and disempower women. While at its heart the gospel is about liberation, and uses the language of redemption from slavery to explain the message of salvation, many of its cultural and ecclesial forms as well as its social behaviour have been infected by the patriarchal patterns of power and domination. Conjure up instead the picture of Gladys Aylward preaching the gospel to women in China, and while she unwrapped the bound feet of her new women friends, singing Charles Wesley's hymn 'And can it be that I should gain':

My chains fell off, my heart was free;
I rose, went forth, and followed thee.

There is a biblical image which may be helpful to European Christians whose relationship to their surrounding culture has changed from being a directive to being a countersign. It is an image which many American Christians are exploring afresh. Christians living in an unrestrained capitalist and military society have begun to perceive themselves as 'living in Babylon'. This is nothing to do with Puritan condemnation of the Roman Church as the 'whore of Babylon' in the seventeenth century. Rather it is criticizing our own enveloping and material society, despite its Christian accoutrements and roots, for being opposed to the heart of the gospel, of being corrupted by power.

The people of Israel understood that they had become exiled captives in Babylon because of the total decay of their relationship with God. The kings of Judah and Israel had both failed. The descendants of King David had not kept the covenant; the people's trust that there would simply always be a descendant of David ruling over them had proved false. King Zedekiah was blinded and carried off to Egypt, the prophecies of doom which Jeremiah the prophet foresaw were fulfilled, and so the people were carried off to Babylon to be subdued and used in a foreign land. By the waters of Babylon they sat down and wept. 'How can we sing the Lord's song in a strange land?' The song of the Hebrew slaves speaks for all oppressed peoples; it can speak too for Christians in a secular culture.

Transfer that image to the situation of the Church today and the idea of 'the Babylonian captivity of the Church' acquires a new resonance. With the apparent triumph of uncontrolled capitalism, a return to legalistic fundamentalisms in much of Jewry, Islam and Christianity, the question goes out to Christians anew: How shall we sing the Lord's song in a culture which has turned its back on anything that we recognize as Christian? How can we serve Christ when we are slaves of an unjust system? How can we praise God in comfort when Lazarus lies at our door? How do we live our covenant in Christ while surrounded by idolatry?

Archbishop Rowan Williams has reinterpreted in a creative way some words of the eighteenth-century Welsh hymnwriter Ann Griffiths. Ann writes that she wants nothing to do with the empty idols of this world:

Beth sydd imi mwy a wnelwyf	The world is full of masks and fetishes
ag eilunod gwael y llawr?	What is in it for me?[3]

Babylon was for the Israelites a society whose values pointed away from the reality of the transcendent God. It was a society centred on false idols of riches, power, sexuality and violence. The world of masks and fetishes is what Babylon was. Do we recognize it around us?

Bible Study

The heresy of the Samaritans
Luke 9.51–56

> When the days drew near for him to be taken up, he set his face to go to Jerusalem. And he sent messengers ahead of him. On their way they entered a village of the Samaritans to make ready for him; but they did not receive him, because his face was set toward Jerusalem. When his disciples James and John saw it, they said, 'Lord, do you want us to command fire to come down from heaven and consume them?' But he turned and rebuked them. Then they went on to another village.

It is after the experience of the transfiguration that in St Luke's Gospel Jesus turns to go up to Jerusalem. It is then that he begins to teach his puzzled and worried disciples that his ministry will involve suffering and rejection. When Peter, James and John come down from the Mount of

Transfiguration with Jesus, first they meet the boy with an evil spirit, and then there is an argument about which of them was the most important. The response of Jesus is to take a child as an illustration of who is most important in the kingdom. Not because a child is 'innocent' but because a child is vulnerable and in that society had none of what we call 'rights'. This is followed by John's anxiety about another healer driving out demons in the name of Jesus, one who was not 'one of us'. Jesus responds with the infrequently quoted sentence, 'Do not stop him, for whoever is not against you is for you.'

The evangelist has laid a trail of clues indicating how important the issue of power and status was, even among those nearest to Jesus. The ground is set for an episode, which should, in the Church, have been the touchstone for any discussion on heresy or deviant thinking. As they pass through Samaria, because their journey is to Jerusalem, the Samaritans reject them. James and John – the sons of thunder – demand, 'Lord do you want us to call fire down from heaven to destroy them?' They had just seen the transfigured Jesus in the presence of Elijah, who had triumphantly brought fire down on the prophets of Baal.

The heresy of the Samaritans was that they had always refused to go along with the centralization of the cult in Jerusalem. They clung to an earlier cultural pattern in which God could be worshipped elsewhere – particularly on their own holy mountain, Mount Gerizim. The building of the temple in Jerusalem by King Solomon at an apparently neutral site, chosen by his father King David, was not universally approved. It identified the worship of Yahweh closely with the power of the king and the court, and indeed of the imperial machine. While King David's time was remembered with affection and the time of King Solomon as a time of great national prestige, it was also remembered as a time of forced labour and a renewed experience of slavery by the ordinary people. The ordinary people no doubt clung to their former patterns of worship.

Further drastic reform was enforced in the time of King Josiah when local shrines were demolished because they were identified with pagan shrines. The reclaiming of the Book of the Law, fortuitously found in the temple, led to a reordering of worship and the demolition of pagan shrines. The prophet Jeremiah supported that reform, but realized that it was inadequate, and that the law needed to be written in people's hearts. 'They have forsaken the spring of living water and have dug their own cisterns, broken cisterns that cannot hold water' (Jer. 2.13). The prophet mocked a people who thought that reform of the temple was enough, people who said, 'We have the temple of the Lord, the temple of the Lord, the temple of the Lord' (Jer. 7.4).

The Samaritans regarded the Law of Moses as what the Lord demanded, and so did not regard the cult at Jerusalem as valid for them. This was why Orthodox Judaism regarded them with such disdain, a feeling which the disciples shared. The disdain was mutual. The Samaritans in this narrative perceive Jesus as just another Jew pushing the rights of the centralized cult and will have nothing to do with him. The disciples respond vindictively, but it is they who are rebuked by Jesus, not the Samaritans. Bringing down fire on those who disagree with us, even when they seem to be rejecting Jesus himself, is not what Jesus requires of us.

When the disciples refer to Elijah there is the possibility that this appeared to be a valuable shred of evidence to people who understood Jesus as the prophet Elijah returned to Israel. Not only was Elijah one of the two figures who appeared to Jesus on the Mount of Transfiguration, his was one of the names quoted when Jesus asked the disciples, 'Who do people say I am?' So it may well be that part of the meaning of this episode is to make it clear that this is not who Jesus is. Bringing down fire to destroy prophets, even if they are false and heretical prophets, is not what Jesus has come to do. The one described in the book of Revelation as 'The Lamb slaughtered from the foundation of the world' does not, unlike Elijah, make a holocaust of human beings. But down the centuries people have felt it necessary to imitate the sons of thunder and behave as though Jesus encouraged our thirst for vengeance.

Christians down the centuries have persistently failed to take to heart the radical message of humility required of those who are, with Jesus, 'Jerusalem bound', called not to the power of the cult, but to challenge the cult to a renewed holiness. It is the way of the cross, for Jesus' condemnation is not for those who refuse him, but for those who protect their religious system before God. Nonetheless, when our cultures collapse, whether from inner corruption or external oppression, the results can be appalling. The account of the healing of the Gerasene demoniac is particularly significant.

The Gerasene Demoniac
Luke 8.26–39 (Matt. 8.28–34; Mark 5.1–20)

> Then they arrived at the country of the Gerasenes, which is opposite Galilee. As he stepped out on land, a man of the city who had demons met him. For a long time he had worn no clothes, and he did not live in a house but in the tombs. When he saw Jesus, he fell down before him and shouted at the top of his voice, 'What have you to do with me, Jesus, Son of the Most High God? I beg you, do not torment me' – for Jesus had commanded the unclean

spirit to come out of the man. (For many times it had seized him; he was kept under guard and bound with chains and shackles, but he would break the bonds and be driven by the demon into the wilds.) Jesus then asked him, 'What is your name?' He said, 'Legion'; for many demons had entered him. They begged him not to order them to go back into the abyss.

Now there on the hillside a large herd of swine was feeding; and the demons begged Jesus to let them enter these. So he gave them permission. Then the demons came out of the man and entered the swine, and the herd rushed down the steep bank into the lake and was drowned.

When the swineherds saw what had happened, they ran off and told it in the city and in the country. Then people came out to see what had happened, and when they came to Jesus, they found the man from whom the demons had gone sitting at the feet of Jesus, clothed and in his right mind. And they were afraid. Those who had seen it told them how the one who had been possessed by demons had been healed. Then all the people of the surrounding country of the Gerasenes asked Jesus to leave them; for they were seized with great fear. So he got into the boat and returned. The man from whom the demons had gone begged that he might be with him; but Jesus sent him away, saying, 'Return to your home, and declare how much God has done for you.' So he went away, proclaiming throughout the city how much Jesus had done for him.

In the Bible study sections it has been stressed several times how ideas, images and themes from the Old Testament, are woven into the New Testament. It has become the approved custom recently to speak of the Hebrew Scriptures and the

Christian Scriptures, and themes from the Hebrew Scriptures are constantly used by Jesus and woven by the evangelists into the Gospel reflections. They belong together. The way Jesus himself used Scripture as the basis of his relationship with God is seen in the temptation narrative, in the way he quotes from the Law of Moses. The books of the prophets are a rich source of images, particularly the book of the prophet Isaiah. The mysterious suffering servant poems, in particular, were used by the early Church to interpret the meaning of the life and death of Jesus. It seems likely that this goes back to Jesus himself, using them to counterbalance the concept of Messiah, which he himself avoided, warning his disciples against using it because it would be misunderstood. This was all part of that explosion of creative energy and theological rethinking that formed the faith of the early resurrection community. The story of the journey to Emmaus in Luke 24.13–35 conveys it as if it all happened in a single afternoon and evening. But there was certainly an extended period of time when the disciples reflected on what happened with Jesus in the light of what the prophets had said. The whole process of searching the Scriptures was done in the light of the resurrection.

We do not always pick up the scriptural references in the Gospels, but when we read this story of the Gerasene demoniac we need to pick up the reference to these verses in Isaiah 65.1–5:

> I was ready to be sought out by those who did not ask; to be found by those who did not seek me. I said, 'Here I am, Here I am,' to a nation that did not call on my name, I held out my hands all day long to a rebellious people, who walk in a way that is not good following their own devices; a people who provoke me to my face con-

tinually, sacrificing in gardens and offering incense on bricks; who sit inside tombs and spend the night in secret places, who eat swine's flesh with broth of abominable things in their vessels; who say 'Keep to yourself, do not come near me, for I am too holy for you.'

The way the demoniac's story is told is an excellent example of this reflective and allusive process. What the Gospel writers knew of God through the Scriptures, they brought to bear on what had happened to them, and sometimes their understanding of the meaning of events is translated into significant detail in the account of that event. It is a story which, if you take it entirely literally, troubles our fact-based approach to narrative. The story is obviously told with the words of Isaiah in mind. For the demoniac represents at one level Israel gone mad. He is produced by a society enslaved, cut from its religious, cultural and moral roots driven crazy by the legions of Rome. He is healed and brought back to his right mind by meeting Jesus and he wants to go back with Jesus. But he is told to stay where he is in a community that does not want to change. The driving out of the pigs farmed for sacrifice (like the lambs at the Sheep Gate in Jerusalem) is a threat to their economic well-being. They had no business rearing them!

Our response to this complex story will quickly reveal our concept of how the truth of Scripture works. It will sort out our perception of how truth is conveyed especially in a narrative. For 'normal' sensible, post-enlightenment twenty-first-century Christians, the story seems to be about evil spirits, and will therefore be a stumbling block. In all the Gospel narratives Jesus sends his disciples to 'cast out demons', even though Jesus told the disciples not to rejoice that the spirits recognized their authority, but rather that their names were written in heaven.

The very existence of 'spirits' at all has been a sharp divide between liberal and conservative Christians. In so-called charismatic churches, the whole issue of spirits and demons becomes a touchstone for accepting the continuing validity of exorcism. What we cannot control in our own individual and social behaviour becomes focused in an 'evil spirit'. Not surprisingly there has been a polarization of attitudes, because the culture we live in does not think that way. Mainline medicine holds that mental illness is caused by chemical imbalance or aberrant electrical activity in the synapses of the brain. Even on the wilder shores of alternative medicine it is assumed there must be some kind of physical imbalance in bodily processes. Liberals identify evil in structures and in sin, while charismatics appear to promote a view of the universe, which is now alien to modern western culture and may well be dismissed as medieval. Although it causes fewer problems in pre-enlightenment cultures particularly in Africa, that is not in the West seen as much of a recommendation.

Is it possible in this, as in other matters of language about the spiritual, to move beyond the old definitions of conservative and liberal, so as to tackle with urgency the world as it is experienced now, as it was experienced in the time of Jesus and as it is described in the New Testament? It may in some instances be perfectly fair to insist that a particular healing miracle was dealing with an example of epilepsy or psychosis. We are more comfortable in interpreting such suffering in terms of mental illness and of treating it with chemicals. But the idea of evil still bothers us. We do not want to think of the world as a struggle between God and the devil and his minions (even though we might enjoy *The Screwtape Letters* of C. S. Lewis). When the media use the term 'evil' to describe child-murderers as well as the murderers of children, or a tyrant whose oppressive and cruel actions have currently become the object of their attention, it sets up great anxiety in a society which is reluctant to use words like 'wrong' or 'wicked', and certainly does not accept the concept of sin or sinfulness. Even when wickedness is obvious, the very idea of evil seems to be essentially religious. The secular media resist that but still want the resonance of the 'language of evil'. Evil is inexplicable to the average, law-abiding citizen who does not at all believe in evil spirits or in God, but who cannot account for behaviour so damaging, so deeply disturbed and disturbing. Language of God and the demonic slithers around in discussions about crime and punishment and in the 'mad or bad' debate.

Yet the popularity of science-fiction, of Buffy the Vampire-Slayer and the X-Files, of 'supernatural' explanations, show that our experience of suffering and evil is not adequately described in terms of drug therapy. Twenty-first-century media watchers and first-century pig breeders may have a different understanding of the world, but it actually is the same world, a world fouled up by evil and failure, which we cannot adequately explain. Is it adequate to describe that in terms of a world swarming with demons? Or are we bound to submit to the materialist assumption that such a view is primitive and unhelpful, ultimately trivializing the results of human sin? For here it looks as if we have to make a choice: either we say, 'Yes, there were demons', which Jesus cast out or which he believed he cast out; or we stick with claiming that here was someone who was acutely sick and damaged, perhaps a case of multiple personality caused by trauma. The rest is accretions, an event touched up with references to Isaiah and the pigs and the gravestones, all foul and 'unclean'.

The American scholar Walter Wink[4] has written

challengingly on the language of spiritual power, on powers, authorities, spirits, demons, angels and gods in the New Testament. He considers the famous passage in the letter to the Ephesians (6.10–12), where the author asserts that our battle is not with human beings but with 'powers and authorities' in the heavenly places. He sets that side-by-side with the perception that we are struggling with systems that need reforming. His analysis of the Gergasene-Gerasene-Gadarene demoniac is one, which enables liberals and conservative to interpret the story afresh.

It may seem glib to make fun of the names issue, but there is a real problem. Gadara is 5 miles and Gerasa 30 miles from the sea of Galilee. Neither place has a shore or cliff. But whichever the place, it seems clear that these events happened somewhere on the south-east shore of the Sea of Galilee in the region of the Decapolis. This was once Greek territory, consisting of ten proud Greek cities founded or enlarged by Alexander the Great and his successors. Gerasa boasted a temple to Zeus, to whom pigs were sacrificed, and a temple dedicated to the cult of Caesar. These were cities, which had been pillaged by both Jews and Romans. It was an area that had lost its freedom to the Ptolemies, to the Seleucids, then to the Romans. Both the gentiles and the Jews suffered there, subject to Rome for tribute and conscription. The Romans kept a legion there until the third century AD. The demoniac is a product of a ravaged society, and the evil apparently concentrated in him is called Legion. In the (London-)Derry Bogside such a madman might be called Union Jack; in Muslim Bosnia he might be called Christian. Imagine what such a deranged individual might be called in Rwanda, on a Navajo reservation, or among the Kurds of northern Iraq. He is driven out of society to live in a place that is unclean and unacceptable to normal society. This interpretation by

Walter Wink of that episode in the ministry of Jesus shows just how relevant the story is to the issue of violence, 'the war against terrorism'.

The Gospels do not present us with a critique of the Roman empire. They are not an attack on Roman authority – indeed the Gospel writers blame the Jews rather than the Romans for the rejection of Jesus. The empire is simply a tool by which that exclusion of Jesus is accomplished. They are the ones who should have known better – though by their own judgement they had not done so in the past. In the story of the Roman centurion we have a glimpse of the benign face of Rome, a man of honour and authority who nonetheless puts aside his own authority in order to acknowledge the different authority and power of Jesus.

The people in the Decapolis lived under the rule of Rome, conforming to the gods of Rome, tied into the economic system and sanctions of Rome. The fact that they are keeping pigs at all is evidence of this. It is not clear in the Gospel whether this is for ritual sacrifice by the Romans or merely a part of the agricultural process. Bear in mind that it was the Prodigal Son who came to his senses when feeding pigs. In that case the pigs are a symbol of his descent into filth and meaninglessness. It was with pigs that he hit rock bottom. Both Jews and Roman used sacrificial ritual. Here Jesus is calling people back into their own covenant, abandoned not for religious reasons but the opposite, out of despair, in exchange for material comfort, for physical survival. And the people reject him like those in Isaiah 65 who say, 'Keep to yourself, do not come near me, for I am too holy for you.'

Topographical or geographical details are often symbolic in the Gospels. Where is the cliff in Nazareth from which it is said that Jesus was nearly driven by the angry mob? There is no such cliff, but for the purpose of the story in Luke 4.29–30 it is the place of destruction, the place from which the scapegoat is driven to die. The mob wanted to get rid of Jesus because he endangered their society and their own self-understanding – thus pointing forward to the cross.

The myth of the scapegoat must be understood in the context of the sacrificial system of the Jewish temple, and of other sacrificing religions in which the sins of people are attributed to, so to speak loaded onto the back an animal, which is driven out into the desert to die.[5] It is a way of getting rid of evil from a society and giving it a fresh start. The idea has been popularized in family counselling, where families are helped to understand ways in which they may have blamed all their problems on one particular child who is perceived to be the troublemaker. Parents and the other children conspire to be the innocent parties; it is, of course, called 'scapegoating'.

Jesus is told to leave them, for having healed the madman, he is now the one to blame, the scapegoat, the one who threatens the society with change, who might undermine their culture and economy with constraints that have been abandoned.

Questions

1 Does the idea of 'living in Babylon' say anything about your situation?

2 In what way is your Christian system untrue to Christ?

3 Where is there decay, change and betrayal in your cultural context?

4 Who would you like to drive out?

5 In your work, is there something, which contradicts your Christian faith? Does that drive you mad? Does anyone regard you as mad?

6 What role does economic necessity play in making us abandon Christian principle?

7 When and where do you rely on Mammon?

8 What difficulties does a Christian industrialist have to face?

Past, Present and Future

During the Second World War the disciplines of security, watchfulness and suspicion become part of the propaganda on the Home Front. Is your journey really necessary? Careless talk costs lives . . . Signposts were taken down lest they help invading troops or carefully planted spies. In Pembrokeshire the news went around that a watchful farmer had spotted a German spy, making enquiries about farm names. In an episode that recalls *Dad's Army*, Home Guard procedures ensured the arrest of this suspicious character who, it was claimed, spoke Welsh with a Berlin accent.

The facts of the case were that a local poet, a teacher, had gone for a walk one Sunday afternoon in spring, and had spent his time 'suspiciously', enjoying the new lambs and the flowers in the hedgerows. Passing the time of day with a local farmer in his yard, he enquired about the name of the farm. The farmer, well-trained in government propaganda, shouted to his brother in the house that there was an odd man around. He demanded the teacher's name. The poet, faced with undeserved hostility, in a quirk of stubbornness refused to give his name. In no time the farmer reported the odd man to the parish priest who rang the constable, who rang the sergeant, so that the following Wednesday the poet-schoolmaster was asked to show his identity card. The tale was a subject for much merriment locally, especially after the culprit explained himself in a poem entitled *Fel hyn y bu* ('This is how it happened'):

Disgrifiwyd y gwrthrych:	The subject was described;
ei ddannedd yn brin	not many teeth and on his
A'i dafod – iaith Dyfed	tongue – language of Dyfed
ac acen Berlin;	but a Berlin accent;
Ei gerdded yn garcus	he walks carefully
rhag ofn yr Home Guard,	in fear of the Home Guard,
A'i osgo fel dyn	and moves warily like a
heb Identity Card.	man without an Identity Card.[1]

The English phrases Home Guard and Identity Card stick out of the Welsh original, comic symbols of hostile and alien values disrupting a rural community, which is normally well-tuned to spotting strangers. The poet goes on to make fun of the constable in Maenclochog and the sergeant in Letterston, who worked away for two whole days before finally identifying the culprit 'spy' between the schoolhouse and the schoolyard.

The intrusion in time of war of such symbolic silliness is comic but needle-sharp. Waldo Williams, Quaker schoolteacher, poet and prophet was one of the finest Welsh poets of the twentieth century. He was brought up in the 1920s in a family that spoke no Welsh, though in a community which was Welsh-speaking. His father was a village schoolmaster from south of the *landsker*, the boundary between the southern, English-speaking part of Pembrokeshire and the Welsh-speaking north. Waldo learned Welsh, and by the time he reached university at Aberystwyth he was part of the Welsh-speaking community of students, although English was his field of study.

Waldo had an impish sense of fun; he particularly

enjoyed pointing out how emperors have no clothes. His innocence was not merely childlike; he enjoyed teasing pomposity and disclosing lies. Perhaps he perceived himself as a bit of an outsider, crossing a boundary not only from a different language, but also from a different world-view. He would compose poems for local eisteddfodau, which deliberately broke the bardic rules, poking fun at the system. There was in him something of the 'holy fool' that might even account for the poor farmer's suspicions! Caring little for comfort, indifferent to the cautions of respectability, he had merry eyes and ready tears. He was a pacifist and conscientious objector. In the 1950s he refused to pay income tax because some of the money would be spent on nuclear armaments. Eventually the bailiffs arrived to take away possessions worth rather more than the amount of tax owed. He was polite and mild-mannered, until one of them asked to borrow a pair of pliers to remove carpet tacks; only then did his patience run out.

Waldo's merriment came from his ability to see through things. He wrote bouncy verses for the local newspaper as well as mystical and symbolic poems that resonate with the mystery of our experience of God. His humour, his faith, and his mysticism irradiate his love of humanity, of Wales, his love of the language he had chosen to write in and its poetic tradition. He was a member of Plaid Cymru, the Party of Wales, attending the party's summer school where in the 1950s and 60s he spent much time nurturing aspiring writers and poets of the younger generation rather than discussing how to run an election campaign. He once stood for election to Westminster for the Pembrokeshire con-stituency, though it is difficult to imagine what he would have done if he had been elected.

One of his simpler poems is entitled *Cofio* ('Remember-ing'). It is a reflection on history, not as a story of kings and generals, armies and kingdoms but as the collective experience of humanity, the little forgotten things of our creatureliness lost in the dust of the past. The civilizations of the past, great palaces and cottages, the destroyed epics and the gods that no one knows about any more. Among the lost treasures are the languages, which have already died, leaving no trace of the communities that spoke them.

A geiriau bach hen	the little words of
ieithoedd diflanedig,	ancient vanished tongues –
Hoyw yng ngenau	lively in the mouths
dynion oeddynt hwy,	of men were they,
A thlws i'r glust ym	and in the speech of children
mharabl plant bychain,	sweet to the ear
Ond tafod neb ni	but no tongue calls
eilw arnynt mwy.	upon them anymore.

All the treasures of human communities, their divine dream and brittle divinity – does anything remain? From Waldo there is the subtlest hint that these treasures remain in the memory of God; that because they have existed in his sight and in his love, they exist eternally, even though human beings destroy and forget them.

Our society and its rapid changes is much concerned about conservation and a bureaucratic 'heritage' industry has made what is old a sort of idol. After the Second World War when so much was destroyed, the rebuilding that happened in British cities was on the whole tatty, unimaginative and utilitarian, and the destruction continued into the 1960s. More was lost through redevelopment than through the bombs of Hitler. But it is much easier to preserve buildings and monuments than to protect people, communities and languages. A sharp-eyed nineteenth-century satirist in Wales, Robert Ambrose Jones (always known as Emrys ap Iwan) identified language as a political issue at a time when many Welsh people and certainly most English people would have agreed with Matthew Arnold that it would be better for all concerned for the Welsh language to die as soon as possible. But, remarked Emrys ap Iwan, we go to great lengths to preserve old, dead buildings like Denbigh castle; why do we not think it right to defend languages which down the centuries have grown into a distinctive way of understanding human experience?

The heritage industry is not, of course, confined to Britain. It is a resource for the global tourist industry. In south-west France, near St Bertrand de Comminges in the Pyrenees, stands the tenth or eleventh-century church of St Juste, incorporating a good deal of Roman stonework. In recent years it has been much repaired and restored. Like many churches in the countryside in the British Isles it is no longer used for worship, even though the graveyard is still in use. Churches of historic interest are cared for by the state in France and the building is in good condition. It is used for concerts, has a fine organ for recitals and chamber music. It is an intriguing example of European heritage, and certainly suggests to the casual visitor the idea that the Christian faith has been rooted in that province for nearly 2,000 years; do not the old stones, the little churchyard surrounding them, speak of the centuries of Christendom? Such an assumption would be inaccurate, for though the Christian faith reached these parts quite early, there was a long gap when the faith in the area was wiped out after the withdrawal of the Roman army, and the church was unused. It was a very different military and ecclesiastical hierarchy that restored a church presence when St Bertrand built the remarkable church up on the hill four miles away at St Bertrand de Comminges.

The builders of St Juste cannibalized the resources that

lay before them. The villas which had been scattered through the area in the time of the empire provided pillars and decorative stones, which told fables and myths and stories of the gods. Stones, apparently depicting Roman tales, were used to illustrate biblical stories. When the figures could not be adapted and renamed, the pagan carving was turned into the wall, and the flat stone merged with the rest of the wall. Tiles and doorways, lumps of stone, carvings, bits of Roman brick, are all reused in the intricacies of a building, which illustrates the way cultures, and faith ebbed and flowed in that part of France.

This was the area of the Albigensian persecutions and wars, when religion and zealotry were all tangled up in this area with political agendas; the French monarchy, centred on Paris, was thrusting down from the north to collide with a defensive 'Pays d'Oc' in the south. Are these wrongs and joys, as Waldo Williams hopes, held in the mind and memory of the eternal God? The beauty of the little building of Saint Juste, the music played there, the liturgy celebrated up the hill in the glorious Romanesque interior of St Bertrand – do they speak to the citizenry in the surrounding countryside?

Another artist of Welsh extraction was deeply intrigued by the kaleidoscope of Roman, Greek, pagan, Nordic, Saxon and Celtic survivals, like *tesserae* in a mosaic, which constitute our European heritage. David Jones, painter and poet, was intensely aware of his Welsh roots, and of the 'accidental' nature of the survival of Welsh in the north-east corner of Wales from which his father came to London. He was fascinated by London itself, the layers of life gone by hidden under the modern pavements of the city. David Jones was a convert to Roman Catholicism, and the Mass itself became for him the central focus holding all the Christian past in the present. His poetry and pictures are

crowded with references and quotations. His vision is of the
faith leaving its symbols and sacramental signs scattered in
stone and wood in landscape and buildings, in song and
poetry, in myths and experiences down the centuries, which
were always God's centuries too.

One of David Jones's greatest paintings, *Vexilla Regis*, is
in the Kettle Yard gallery in Cambridge. It works rather like
an icon, if some basic explanation is given. Art critics find
the need for explanation a weakness, but the painting does
address in an original way the issues of mortality and
evanescence, of permanence and change, of looking back
and looking forward, and looking into an eternity in which
there is neither time nor space. It is initially an uncomfortable exercise in humility and challenges us to a new perspective in our attitude to the past.[2] The painting gets it title
Vexilla Regis from a sixth-century Good Friday hymn by
Venantius Fortunatus, one of the many hymns translated in
the nineteenth century by J. M. Neale:

> The royal banners forward go,
> the Cross shines forth in mystic glow . . .
>
> O Tree of glory, Tree most fair,
> ordained those holy limbs to bear . . .
>
> as by the Cross thou dost restore
> so rule and guide us evermore.

David Jones wrote that:

> The main jumping off ground was I think a Latin hymn
> we sing as part of the Good Friday liturgy in the Roman
> rite. Two hymns in fact, one starting Vexilla Regis
> prodeunt . . . and the other starting Crux fidelis . . . a

rather long hymn dealing with the cross as a tree in concise and very noble and moving language.

The three trees in the painting are the three crosses of Calvary, as though they had been left standing where they were planted. It puts in visual form the fanciful idea that the cross on which Christ was crucified took root and continued to grow. The central tree thus stands forth magnificent and strong. The tree on the left is the one on which the good thief was crucified. In it David Jones placed a pelican pecking its breast to feed its young, a favourite church icon of piety. On the right there is a tree trunk, which *is partly a column and is the cross of the unrepentant thief*. It is, says David Jones:

> partly tree and partly triumphant column and partly imperial standard – a power symbol, it is not rooted to the ground, but rather is held in place by wedges. St Augustine's remark that 'empire is great robbery' influenced me here. It is not meant to be bad in itself but in some sense proud and self-sufficient.[3]

In the bottom left-hand corner there is a leopard's pelt and trumpet, signifying the instrument and insignia of a Roman trumpeter, as if the owner had been part of the guard at Calvary. David Jones, who fought as a private in the First World War, was always fascinated by the figure of the soldier, and his long poem *In Parenthesis* deals with the vivid human individuality of soldiers, identifying the archetypal similarity between the Roman soldiers on Hadrian's wall and the guards of the First World War. In another painting a young soldier dressed in soldier's greatcoat is caught on a thicket of barbed wire, along with a lamb, which is at the same time the lamb found by Abraham to take the place of Isaac, and Jesus, proclaimed the Lamb of God by John the Baptist. *Vexilla Regis* is about the survival of the cross as a symbol of life down the centuries and it is about the collapse and fragmentation of cultures. Bits of the Roman world, pillars and broken temples like those incorporated in the church of St Juste are scattered about, and far in the distance Celtic hill-forts show how far the story of the cross has reached.

At times of war, at moments of obvious historic resonance as well as in the smaller domestic crises of change and decision, there is always a question of letting go the past. The dilemma is well-illustrated by a parable from South Africa. At the time when the apartheid regime was at its height a group of social workers in Capetown were looking after street children. They had a refuge with facilities for welcoming the children, providing them with food, clothing and safety. One day a worker brought in a boy of about six years old. The child had been looking for food, foraging in the waste bins at the back of the building. He was frightened and angry; he was filthy, ragged and starving. Talked to gently, he relaxed a little and made no great objection to being washed and cleaned up, positively welcomed a new pair of shorts and T-shirt. But while all this was happening his left hand was held tightly clenched in a fist. He could not be persuaded to open his hand to have it washed or to reveal what it was that he held so tight. Finally he was taken into the canteen where there was a great choice of food prepared: bread and meat, vegetables and an abundance of fruit, milk to drink. Yes, it was explained, he could have anything he liked. Only then did he agree to opening his fist and putting down the squashed and grimy crust of bread that was all he had picked up at the bins.

That story, told by Archbishop Bill Burnett, former

Archbishop of Capetown, provides a vivid instance of human distrust of the future. It shows how, when our experience is limited and painful, we cannot envisage anything better. What we have is our treasure and we will hang on to it. We have the gravest difficulty in turning away from things past and looking to the future. It is the consistent plea of the prophet Isaiah to his people. God is not confined to repeating himself. He can do new things. The folk wisdom of the Jews in the book of Ecclesiastes says: *Do not say 'Why were the former days better than these?' For it is not from wisdom that you are ask this* (7.10).

In the book of Ezra (chapter 3) there is a description of the people of Israel rebuilding the walls of Jerusalem and the temple. Those who remembered the temple in its former glory were deeply distressed because it had nothing of the beauty that they remembered. But the younger generation, who had never seen any temple at all, were filled with delight at the new temple and its promise for the future. So the place resounded with the weeping of the old and the delighted laughter of the young; there was so much noise that you could not tell which was which. It is a tragi-comic picture of the fracture between generations and the difference of approach between the young and the old. But the prophetic voice consistently points forward. Look to God who leads you into the future; there in the future promise is the seed of the resurrection faith of the New Testament.

The question that arises for those of us who hang on to their heritage 'at the turn of a civilization' is the issue of the cost of following Jesus. It was the question for individual apostles. It was the question with which Paul struggled, and the issue that caused the fracture of the early Church after it had managed for a short time to contain both Jewish and gentile Christians. Many find faith unimaginable except in the familiar and loved rituals of church and home, where faith and culture are inextricably woven together. It is painful to consider that the gospel, that God, does not depend on the rags and tatters of culture; to find that the very best which we can imagine as our sacrifice of praise and faithful living can come between us and the eternal mercy of God. The fragility of our most precious treasures and relationships needs to be held very lightly before God. To come empty-handed is the most seemly.

In the previous chapter we considered the issue of the Samaritans who refused to respond to the Jesus who was Jerusalem-bound. Immediately following that section is one of the grittiest and harshest of collections of the sayings of Jesus. Gathered together they show the response of Jesus to people he suspected of only partial, superficial or ill-considered commitment. And they indicate the kinds of excuses that people gave for not responding to Jesus, for not persevering in their discipleship. For the Samaritans it was a long-standing resistance and resentment of orthodox Jewry and Jerusalem as the centre of the cult. It was an unwillingness to go along with what they felt was an essentially Jewish agenda. They could see Jesus only as a Jew. But 'Jerusalem' for Jesus is not merely the centre of the cult, the temple, the symbol of the nation; rather it is a symbol of his own coming passion and death, the catastrophe that ends his human life. It is the place over which he weeps because it is the place that has stoned the prophets and which still cannot read the signs of the times and cannot understand those things which make for the peace of God. The 'journey to Jerusalem' is not one which can be drawn on a map; it cannot be timed and historicized. It must be conceived as a journey into darkness and abandonment, a journey into rejection, because of his total obedience to the values of the kingdom of God. It is part of the passion story; the weakness of would-be disciples as well as apparently committed disciples is part of the suffering of Jesus. That is the context for the episode in Samaria and it is just as important in understanding the next section in which Jesus is apparently, warning off would-be disciples.

Bible Study

Luke 9.57–62 (Matt. 8.19–22)[4]

> As they were going along the road, someone said to him, 'I will follow you wherever you go.' And Jesus said to him, 'Foxes have holes, and birds of the air have nests; but the Son of Man has nowhere to lay his head.'

> To another he said, 'Follow me.' But he said, 'Lord, first let me go and bury my father.' But Jesus said to him, 'Let the dead bury their own dead; but as for you, go and proclaim the kingdom of God.'

> Another said, 'I will follow you Lord, but let me first say farewell to those at my home.' Jesus said to him, 'No one who puts a hand to the plough and looks back is fit for the kingdom of God.'

Luke presents here a group of three sayings in which Jesus seems to be virtually discouraging people from being disciples. The answers he gives are so severe that some have been tempted to suggest that these sayings were from an early rigorist sect that allowed no room for family or cultural commitment in followers of Jesus. This seems a rather devious way of avoiding what is being said. Jesus has reached a point in his ministry when he does not need hangers-on, admirers or people wanting to manipulate him into their agendas. Under a darkening sky, moving forward to Jerusalem, Jesus is increasingly aware of the cost for himself, and so he warns the disciples of the cost to them. In Matthew there are just two exchanges: one to do with the Son of Man not having a place to lay his head, and the other to do with letting the dead bury their dead. In Luke there is an additional excuse about not counting the cost in advance and the uselessness of setting your hand to the plough and looking back.

The first is about not having a home, about insecurity:

> As they were going along the road, someone said to him, 'I will follow you wherever you go.' And Jesus said to him, 'Foxes have holes, and birds of the air have nests; but the Son of Man has nowhere to lay his head.'

You would expect Jesus to welcome the enthusiasm of 'I will follow you wherever you go.' But they are only words, good intentions and wind. 'Someone' does not appear to be a new follower but one who is already part of the circle of disciples 'going along the road' with Jesus. This is not a new devotee, but someone who has been inspired to make a more unconditional commitment. Jesus does not encourage but seems rather to pour cold water on his good intentions. The crowds of his early ministry of healing in Galilee are perhaps already falling away. He does not really want popularity, a fair-weather crowd milling around him. Therefore he does not encourage anyone with false promises of security. There are already too many disciples with false expectations of success and desires of what a Messiah might do for them. Jesus frequently has to deal with the misunderstandings of the disciples, their hopes of influence, political effectiveness, and a place at 'his right hand'. Jesus judges it to be a seed planted among thorns, or on the pathway, good intentions that will disappoint him.

Jesus warns against such easy promises. These are after all the ones who will fall away from him. In the enthusiasm of the company, in the charismatic presence of Jesus, it is the sort of thing that people would say. Jesus might even be saying that this is not a fan club. Think, count the cost, realize what you're getting into – and don't bother me with words.

The band of disciples actually seem not to have been in any great need of anything. They were sustained by a group of relatively moneyed women who accompanied them. They did not go hungry. There were many homes and centres at which they were welcome. They were not mendicants; in fact they were fêted and partied. They were not by any means destitute, but some of them had hopes of great things. Jesus points out that he does not have property, he has nowhere he can call his own as of right, by law. He does not hold title deeds. There is nowhere where 'he can lay his head'; there is no security.

This kind of vulnerability, of trust in God's provision has been a challenge taken up literally at various times. Sometimes it has been to follow Christ like Francis of Assisi. At other times it has been the less dramatic and more boring clerical poverty of humble church ministry. It has been the basis of training in certain kinds of Pentecostal ministry to depend on 'what the Lord provides', especially among the poorest and most needy of young people. Chosen, voluntary poverty has been the proof of solidarity with the needy. That is very different from those who criticize the lack of career prospects in Christian ministry. Jesus says elsewhere, they get their 'wage' (reward), such as it is. It is still possible to miss the gift, the grace, which is on offer.

The kind of spirituality that prays for 'Revival' and even 'Renewal' sometimes feeds on this kind of enthusiasm. The South Wales evangelical revival of 1904–5, whose harvest was decimated by world war and economic depression, brought thousands to faith and many more to emotional excitement. One wary sceptic commented that it was all a fire in straw. The Lord who is Jerusalem-bound rejects impetuous promises.

The second difficulty is quite different:

> To another he said, 'Follow me.' But he said 'Lord, first let me go and bury my father.' But Jesus said to him, 'Let the dead bury their own dead; but as for you, go and proclaim the kingdom of God.'

If we think we are dealing with a particular individual in the throes of grief, with his father's body awaiting burial that afternoon, then we misunderstand what's going on. Jesus would surely be going to the wake rather than making unreasonable demands. The harshness of 'let the dead bury their dead' allows no room for grief or loss, and would surely be inhuman. Jesus is consistently critical of religious laws, which make people behave in an inhuman way; the priest and the Levite in the story of the Good Samaritan are the best examples. Those who criticized the healing of the bent old woman in the synagogue on a sabbath are in that category. Here if the story were taken literally, then surely Jesus would be inhuman in dismissing someone's grief at the death of a father. In the context of the law, burying one's father was a prime religious duty. Having a son to say Kaddish, being a son saying it, was and is a core religious duty. It is a symbol of love within the covenant, of continuity and religious answerability of a new generation before God. Why should Jesus dismiss it?

Again, if the story is about an individual, then more needs to be known about the individual. And we are tempted into the path of speculation. Perhaps this man was lying and his father was simply old and unwell and in no immediate danger of dying. The deferral of discipleship and going on the journey to Jerusalem was not a matter of a day or two, but weeks, months even years. Jesus was demanding urgency. A duty to be fulfilled sometime in the future is not denied by responding to the call of Jesus to follow him now. It might be that the man was using a common expression meaning he didn't want to do something now, immediately. It is suggested that 'Let me first go and bury my father' was an acknowledged way of getting out of something, like 'seeing a man about a dog'. The suggestion is feasible and at least does not distort the point being made, which is that Jesus thinks this individual (or this type) is simply putting things off. Jesus may well have met many such who said 'some day perhaps . . .' If this is correct it is interesting that a specifically religious duty in the culture in which Jesus was brought up, a duty imposed by the law, is used as an excuse for not responding to the call of God now. The immediacy of God's call to us is shunted aside by legality. So to the dilly-dalliers, to the ones who think there is plenty of time, Jesus says that the matter is urgent. There is no time to mess about with non-urgent duties. God has something to say to you now, so your other obligations, even if they appear to be religious or legal ones, do not count. Who then are the dead? Surely they are the whitened sepulchres, the people who used the dead hand of the law, the letter that kills to destroy the vital relationship between God and those who respond to the call. If that is correct then this is another criticism of the Pharisees.

St Augustine tells his own story of deferring his response of faith, his desire to be chaste 'but not yet'. We know that people put off religious decisions, feeling there's plenty of time for that some other day. Research says that people's lives are so busy and pressurized these days that regularity in Sunday worship, for example, has become much more rare. The regular worshipper becomes a once-or-twice-a-monther. It is one option among the other family needs of shopping, sport, sex, clubbing, fun, entertainment, rugby, ballet lessons and the Sunday papers. I will become a follower of Christ when I have passed my exams, got a job, got married, had children, paid off my mortgage, fixed my pension, been on holiday . . . always *after*, always *not yet*. Jesus is highlighting the priority of the call of God. It is either all-important or it is not true; the call of God will not normally enable us to wriggle out of human duties. Sometimes we assume that our ordinary, prosaic church life is all that God is asking of us. We are good at keeping something back for later. Paul puts the point simply to the Corinthians, 'Now is the day of salvation . . .'.

> Another said, 'I will follow you Lord, but let me first say farewell to those at my home.' Jesus said to him, 'No one who puts a hand to the plough and looks back is fit for the kingdom of God.'

This in many ways seems the harshest of the three sayings. Human relationships, family relationships, where there is duty of care and sustenance, are at stake. When Elisha sought to follow Elijah he was allowed to return home to say goodbye to his family (1 Kgs 19.20). Elisha was in many ways a pattern of the passionate and absolutely devoted disciple and follower of the prophet. This episode must be in the mind of the evangelist in including the saying here. Again we find it hard to believe that Jesus did not allow his disciples to say goodbye to their families.

How then do we read this text? The disciples are already on the road to Jerusalem. These are not newcomers but people already committed. These disciples have found that the going is hard, the skies are darkening and they are getting frightened. They feel dread of Jerusalem. They start to remember the attractions of what they have left behind. There are Christians who go through a sort of mid-life crisis. They have committed themselves in youth to the Christian call and in their late forties it all goes dull and sour; they become cynical not only about church, but about their own faith. It is not uncommon for people to look back and wish they hadn't ever started down this path. If they had not taken this path, would not life have been more exciting, more comfortable, and more glamorous? Jesus talks of people who have already 'put their hand to the plough', and so it makes sense to imagine that he is talking about more than one disciple who is getting disillusioned, frightened, even cynical.

Jesus' response therefore is about the need for persistence, for a capacity to live out the results of the perhaps impetuous decision to follow Christ. The image drawn from ploughing is typical of the imagery he uses, rooted in the ordinary lives of the people of his time. Looking back when you are ploughing leads either to an abandoned piece of work or a bad wobble in the pattern of furrows. It means a worker making a public fool of himself, a task badly done or unfinished. Disciples once embarked upon their journey are required by the kingdom of God to have a capacity to keep going, not to seek for opportunities to opt out, not to make ourselves the object of persuasion to stay behind and be distracted by other important things. Changing our priorities is not an option.

These exchanges are set in the context of the journey to Jerusalem, but they stand also as symbolic exchanges in which Jesus is spelling out the cost of being a disciple. Each one is particularly relevant to different stages of our following, but at whatever stage we are, the qualities to which Jesus is drawing us are things we need constantly to bear in mind.

We have to:

- count the cost
- respond with urgency
- be persistent.

The call of Jesus to his disciples appears to be, 'Come follow me. Now. No security in possessions or family, no going back, a consistent sense of urgency.'

Questions

1 What treasure in your heritage do you most value?
2 Which of the three challenges to followers of Jesus is most relevant to you?
3 What promises for the future can answer our sense of loss on Good Friday?

Notes

1. Elin ap Hywel and Grahame Davies, *Ffiniau Borders*, Gomer Press, 2002.

Introduction

1. W. B. Yeats, 'A Prayer for My Daughter', *Collected Works of W. B. Yeats*, London: Simon & Schuster, 2001.

1. Nurse Logs: Trees and Peoples

1. T. Rowland Hughes, *Can neu Ddwy*, 1948.

2. Power and Politics: God on the Boundary

1. The Letter to Diognetus can be found in *The Apostolic Fathers* edited and translated by J. B. Lightfoot. This is my own translation of the text.

2. See 'Ozymandias' in *The Major Works of P. B. Shelley*: Oxford University Press, 2003.

3. Peoples at the Hedge of Thorns

1. This story was told by the Revd Wali Fejo, a Methodist minister from Australia at the international conference organized by the Council for World Evangelism, a section of the World Council of Churches, in El Salvador, Brazil in 1996. The conference had a pre-ponderance of white, western Christians but there were enough minority peoples present to whom the gospel had been preached by mainly nineteenth-century missionaries for their perspective to be the

most important one in the conference. White hostility to campaigns for aboriginal rights is a major political issue in Australia.

2. Vincent Donovan, *Christianity Rediscovered*, London: SCM Press and Maryknoll: Orbis Books, 1993.

3. Hesketh Pearson, *The Smith of Smiths*, London: Hogarth Press, 1984.

4. Anton Wessels, *Europe: Was it Ever Really Christian?*, London: SCM Press, 1994.

5. Waldo Williams, *Dail Pren*, Llandysul: Gwasg Gomer, 1956, 1982.

4. *Between Men and Women*

1. Louise Erdrich, *The Last Report on the Miracles at Little No Horse*, London: HarperCollins 2001.

2. John Fletcher, *The Tamer Tamed*, London: Nick Ham Books, 2003.

3. See Leviticus 15.19: 'When a woman has a discharge of blood that is her regular discharge from her body, she shall be in her impurity for seven days, and whoever touches her shall be unclean until the evening.'

5. *Communicating and Language*

1. Paul D. Garrett, *St Innocent: Apostle to America*, New York: St Vladimir's Press, 1979.

2. See Anton Wessels, *Europe: Was it Ever Really Christian?*, London: SCM Press, 1994.

3. Raymond Brown, *The Birth of the Messiah*, New York: Doubleday, 1977; or in more accessible essays, *The Coming Christ in Advent*, and *An Adult Christ at Christmas*, Minnesota: Liturgical Press, 1988.

6. *Between Public and Personal: The Lament of History*

1. Gary Mason, *Sectarianism and Violence*, CMME Papers, Salvador Bahia.

2. Dr Musimbi Kanyoro at CMME Conference in Salvador, 1996.

3. Ann Griffiths, '*Caneuon Ffydd*' in Rowan Williams, *After Silent Centuries*, Perpetua Press, 2001.

4. Walter Wink, 1. *Naming the Powers: The Language of Power in the New Testament*; 2. *Unmasking the Powers: The Invisible Powers that Determine Human Existence*; 3. *Engaging the Powers: Discernment and Resistance in a World of Domination*, Philadelphia: Augsburg Fortress Press, 1984, 1986, 1992.

5. René Girard, *The Scapegoat*, Maryland: Johns Hopkins University Press, 1986; *Things Hidden since the Foundation of the World*, London: Athlone Press, 1987.

7. *Past, Present and Future*

1. Waldo Williams, *Dail Pren*, Llandysul: Gwasg Gomer, 1956, 1982.

2. It is a point that Jones makes more explicitly in his poem 'A, a, a, domine deus'. How do we in our age, an age of 'nozzles and containers' of mechanics and technicalities, search for God? 'It is easy to miss them at the turn of a civilization.'

3. See Jonathan Miles and Derek Shiel, *David Jones, the Maker Unmade*, Bridgend: Seren, 1995.

4. John Sullivan OP, speaking at the Assembly of Churches Together in Britain and Ireland, was the source of some of the basic ideas in this section.

Index of Subjects and Names

'A, a, a, domine deus'
(David Jones) 165n
Abilete (African chief's son)
119–21
aborigines 49, 163n
Abraham 48–50
Acts, mission within the
early Church 58–9
Aleutian Islands (Alaska),
Orthodox missions
(nineteenth century)
95–7, 98–100
almsgiving 24
Anglican expatriates,
religious culture 7
Anglicanism, author's entry
into xii
anti-semitism 60
Apostles, maleness 77–8
Arnold, Matthew 148
Arthur (British king) 27,
34
Ash Wednesday,
significance 18, 24
Augustine of Hippo, St
116, 117, 126, 127, 159

Aylward, Gladys 129

Babel, effects reversed at
Pentecost 101
Babylon, imagery, used of
society in relation to
Christianity 129–31
Baghdad 33
Balkans, evangelization
103–4
baptism
Masai concepts of as a
community experience
51–2
preparation, evolution
into Lent observance
12–13
use in the slave trade 122
Bardsey Island (Lleyn
peninsula, north west
Wales) 11–12
Barnabas, St (St Paul's
companion) 62, 65
Barr, James 60
Barry, James (Inspector-
General of Her

Majesty's Hospitals in
Montreal: 1850s)
69–70
Bede, Venerable 54
Behring, Nicholas 98
Beowulf 105
Bible, translation into
Welsh 102–3
Bible studies 17–25,
38–46, 60–8, 78–94,
106–18, 131–42,
155–62
biblical references
Genesis, 18 49–50
Exodus, 17.3–7 43
Deuteronomy
6.13 45
6.16 43
8.3 41
1 Kings
7.7–24 109
17 42
19.20 160
2 Kings, 5 109
Ezra, 3 153
Psalms
16.6 xi
62, 22 19
Ecclesiastes, 7.10 153
Isaiah
29.13 88
61 107, 108
65 141
65.1–5 136–7

Jeremiah
2.13 133
7.4–7 87
Matthew
4.1–11 38–46
6.1–6 17
6.16–21 17
8.19–22 155
8.28–34 134
9.18–26 78
15.1–28 84–6
15.21 91
19.16–30 45
23.15 57 56
24 56
Mark
1.12–15 38, 39
5.1–20 134
5.21–43 78–84
Luke
1–2 59
2.29–32 59
4.1–13 38, 39
4.14 106–8
4.18–19 107, 109
4.22 107
4.28–30 110
4.29–30 142
8.26–39 134–42
8.40 78
9.51–6 131
9.57–62 155
11 56
16.19–31 41

18.8–39 45
24.13–35 136
John
  3 67
  6 42
Acts
  10.1–17 60–1, 62
  10.2 62
  10.28 63
  10.34 64
  10.9–22 63
  15 15
  15.22–9 14
1 Corinthians,
  9.20–1 67
Galatians
  1.13–2.21 65
  2.11–14 66
  3.14 66
  3.28 115
  Ephesians, 6.10–12 140
  Philippians, 3.8 1, 59
Brazil, slave trade 122–4
Brychan (father of
  Gwladys, wife of
  Gwynllyw Farfog)
  26–7
Burnett, Bill (formerly
  Archbishop of Cape
  Town) 152–3

cannibalism, Christians
  accused of 30
Celts 35

Chad Varah, Chad
  (founder of the
  Samaritans) 83
Charlemagne 104
children, lack of power and
  status as the Christian
  norm 132
Christian Scriptures, use of
  Hebrew Scriptures
  136–7
Christianity
  accommodation to social
    culture 117–18
  conflicts with African
    tribal cultures 119–21
  cultural conflicts with
    Judaism 1–2, 14–16
  cultural conflicts with
    other religions 1–3
  cultural role as the
    scapegoat 134–42
  and cultural survival
    149–55
  power and status within
    132–4
  values
    clash with cultural values
      119–31
    and not reflected in
      church buildings 124
Christianity Rediscovered
  (Donovan) 53
Church
  conformation to social

culture 117
as exclusive means of
salvation 126–7
see also early Church
church buildings, as
reflections of social
cultural values rather
than Christian values
124
Church/Old Slavonic
language, use in mission
103
Churches Together in
Britain and Ireland
(CTBI) 126
circumcision 14, 15–16,
65
citizenship, Christian
citizenship 30–1
Cofio ('Remembering')
(Waldo Williams)
146–7
Constantine the Great,
conversion, effects on
the Church 31, 35–6
Cornelius (Roman
centurion and God-
fearer) 60–1, 62–4
Council for World Mission
and Evangelism (1996
conference, Salvador
(Bahia, Brazil)) xiii,
122–3, 163n
Crucifixion, titula, and its

significance for mission
101–2
CTBI (Churches Together
in Britain and Ireland)
126
culture
African tribal cultures,
conflicts with
Christianity 119–21
Christianity's role as the
scapegoat within society
134–42
clash with Christian
values 119–31, 124
effect on religious beliefs
7–14, 18–24
and the historical sense
146–7
and mission 95–101,
104–6
and religious divisions
1–5
survival 147–55
Cuthbert, St 36
Cyril, St 103
Cyrillic language, effects on
mission 103

Dark Ages 32, 33–4
David (king of Israel) 132
death, and ritual purity
83–4
demonology, Christian
attitudes to 137–40

discipleship 154–62
Donatism 126, 127
Donovan, Vincent
    (missionary with the
    Masai) 50–2, 53
The Dream of the Rood
    106

early Church
  divisions between Jews
    and gentiles 1–2,
    14–16
  effects of Constantine the
    Great's conversion 31,
    35–6
  equality within 71
  missionary outreach, and
    conflicts with Judaism
    58–60, 64–5
  see also Church
Edwin (British king) 54
Elijah, Jesus likened to
    133–4
Elisha, discipleship 160
Emmaus, journey to 136
Emrys ap Iwan (Robert
    Ambrose Jones) 147–8
Erdrich, Louise (poet and
    novelist) 71–3
Eucharist, reception by the
    Masai 52
evil, concept 138–9

Fall, doctrine 75–6
fasting 22–4

Fejo, Wali (Australian
    Methodist Minister)
    49, 163n
Fel hyn y bu ('This is how it
    happened') (Waldo
    Williams) 145
Fletcher, John (Elizabethan
    playwright) 76–7
food taboos, conflicts
    between early
    Christianity and
    Judaism 15
Francis of Assissi, St 124
Francis Xavier, St 124

gender boundaries, and
    social roles 70–94
gentiles
  Jewish attitudes towards
    89–93
  within Luke's Gospel
    108, 109–13, 113–14
Geresene demoniac
    134–42
Good Samaritan (parable)
    57–8
Greek, use in mission 101,
    102
Griffiths, Ann (eighteenth-
    century Welsh hymn
    writer) 131
Gwladys (wife of
    Gwynllyw Farfog)
    26–7, 28

Gwynllyw Farfog (Welsh
    chieftain and saint)
    26–9, 35
Gymanfa Gana, author
    visits (1997) 6

Hebrew Scriptures, use in
    Christian Scriptures
    136–7
Heliand ('The Saviour')
    105–6
Herbert family (Elizabethan
    settlers in Ireland) 32–3
heretics, lack of rights 127
Herman, St 98–100
Hilda, St 36
Hildegard of Bingen, St
    117
history, sense, and culture
    146–7
homosexuality 91
Hughes, T. Rowland 6
hunger 41–2

In Parenthesis (David
    Jones) 151
India, Anglican expatriates
    and their religious
    culture 7
Innokent, St (John
    Veniaminov) 95–8, 100
interreligious conflicts 128
Iraq war 33
Isaiah, faith in the future
    153

Islam 2–3, 128
Israel
    exodus, as model for
        Christ's temptations
        40–1
    relations with gentiles,
        theme within Luke's
        Gospel 108, 109–13
    see also Judaism

Jairus' daughter, healing
    78–80, 81, 83–4
Jeremiah 13
    welcomes Josianic reforms
        133
Jerusalem, Jesus' pilgrimage
    to 154–5, 156
Jesus Christ
    attitudes to cultural issues
        3, 4
    attitudes towards gentiles
        84, 89–93
    attitudes towards ritual
        purity 85–9
    criticisms of Pharisees'
        attitudes to mission
        56–8, 67–8
    death, as baptism 12
    and discipleship 154–62
    and gender boundaries
        77–84, 92–3
    infancy narratives, as the
        bridging of cultural
        divides 14

portrayal in literature
106
on religious observance
17–24
as the scapegoat 142
sermon in the synagogue
at Nazareth 106
temptations 13, 38–46
transfiguration and
rejection 131–4
use of Hebrew Scriptures
136
Jews for Jesus 60
John the Baptist, St 39
John (manservant to James
Barry) 70
Jones, David (painter and
poet) 149–51
Jones, Jack (Baptist
preacher) 91
Jones, Robert Ambrose
(Emrys ap Iwan) 147–8
Josiah (king of Judah) 133
Judaism
attitudes towards gentiles
84, 89–93
cultural conflicts with
Christianity 1–2,
14–16
and mission 55–60
within the early Church
64–5
religious taboos 84
see also Israel

Justice and Reconciliation
Commission (South
Africa) 113

Kanyoro, Musimbi, Dr
128–9

language
effects on mission 101–6
importance xii, xiii,
147–8
*The Last Report on the
Miracles at Little No
Horse* (Erdrich) 72–5
Latin, use in mission 101,
102
Lent xiii–xiv, 12–13, 18,
22, 24
Leopolda, Sister (in
Erdrich, *Last Report*)
73
Letter to Diognetus 30
Lewis, C. S. 18, 138
Love Medicine (Erdrich)
71–2
Luke, Gospel
portrayal of women 77
themes 106–7, 108
Luther, Martin 102

Makah Indians, culture
suppressed by religious
imperialism 7–9
Marcion 59

Martin of Tours, St 29

Mary Magdalene, St 78

Masai, contacts with Christian missions 50–2

Mason, Gary 125–6, 127

Matthew, Gospel, Jewish background 16, 58–9, 86, 88, 93

menstruation, and ritual purity 81–3

Messianic secret 44

Methodius, St 103

Milton, John 76

mission
  as affected by language 101–6
  in relation to Judaism 55–60, 64–5
  in relation to social cultures 47–57, 66–7, 95–101, 104–6

Modeste, Damien (Roman Catholic priest in Erdrich, *Last Report*) 72–5

monasticism 31

Morgan, Enid, visit to the Makah Indian reservation (1997) 6–9

Moses 43–4

multiculturalism, concept xii

Nanapush (Indian shaman, in Erdrich, *Last Report*) 74

Neale, J. M. 150

Nicodemus (Pharisee) 67–8

Nightingale, Florence 69

Nikolai of Tokyo (first Orthodox priest in Japan) 98

Nonconformists, social power as a result of the disestablishment of the Welsh Church 37

Norman conquest, affects Welsh church organization 32, 34

Northern Ireland, sectarian conflicts 124–8

nurse logs, cultural analogy for the spread of Christianity 10–11

Olympic Peninsula (USA), author visits 7–10

Onesimus (slave) 114–15

Orthodox Churches, receipt of communion by menstruating women 82

Ozymandias 33

patriarchy
  effects on women 2–3

within the early Church
71
Paul, St
on almsgiving 24
attitudes to Jewish
religious culture 1–2,
14–15
concern with slavery
114–15, 116
missionary activity 56,
59–60, 61–2, 64, 65–6,
67
Paulinus, St (missionary to
England) 54
Pentecost, as the reversal of
Babel 101
Peter, St
missionary activity 61,
62, 63–4, 65
overcoming of Jewish
dietary laws 15
Petrucchio (in
Shakespeare's *Taming
of the Shrew*) 76
Pharisees
missionary attitudes
criticized by Christ
56–8, 67–8
opposition to Jesus on the
grounds of ritual purity
86–7, 88
Philemon, Paul's letter to
114–15, 116
piety 18–19

pigs 141
politics, effects on religious
beliefs 26–37, 40–6
power, and status, within
Christianity 132–4
Prado, Luiz, Bishop xiii
prayer 21–2, 23–4
Presbyterianism, and
sectarianism 126–7,
128
priesthood, attitudes
towards menstruation
82
Providence, doctrine 127
purity *see* ritual purity
Pwyll, Pendefig Dyfed 105

reconciliation 116
and slavery 114–15
Reform 127
religious beliefs
as affected by political life
26–37, 40–6
and cultural imperialism
7–12
effects on culture 13–14,
18–24
religious divisions, and
cultural attitudes 1–5
religious imperialism,
suppression of Makah
Indian culture 7–9
religious observance 17–24
religious taboos 84

'Remembering' (*Cofoio*)
(Waldo Williams)
146–7
revenge, human longing
for, Jesus' rejection
110–13
rich young ruler, story
45–6
ritual purity
and death 83–4
Jewish attitudes towards
84–9
and menstruation 81–3
Peter's missionary
outreach in Joppa 62,
63–4
in the story of the Good
Samaritan 57–8
'The River of Separation'
(Navaho myth), on
gender differences and
social roles 76
Roman Catholic Church,
and sectarianism 126
Roman Empire
Christian attitudes to 141
collapse, effects on Britain
34, 36
'Rough Guide' (Grahame
Davies) viii–ix
Russian Missionary Society
97
Russian Orthodox Church
Aleutian mission 95–100

sectarianism 127
Ryn ni yma o hyd ('We're
still here') 8

St Beuno's Roman Catholic
Retreat Centre (North
East Wales) xi, xiii
St Juste church (St Bertrand
de Comminges, France)
148–9, 152
St Woollo's cathedral (Stow
Hill, Newport) 29
saints, Celtic saints 27, 31,
32, 35
Salvador (Bahia, Brazil),
slave trading history
121–4
Samaritans (organization),
foundation 83
Samaritans (people), heresy
131–4, 154
'The Saviour' (*Heliand*)
105–6
scapegoats 142
The Screwtape Letters
(Lewis) 138
Scriptures, Christian use of
Hebrew Scriptures
136–7
Seattle, author visits (1997)
6–7
Second World War,
security measures
144–5

sectarianism, Northern
    Ireland 124–8
Shakespeare, William 76
Shelley, Percy Bysshe 33
Shra Castle (Ireland) 32
slavery
  Brazil 122–4
  imagery, used in the
    doctrine of salvation
    129
  and reconciliation 114–15
Smith, Sidney (missionary
    in India) 53
social culture, Christianity's
    accommodation with
    117–18
social roles, and gender
    boundaries 70–94
Solomon (king of Israel)
    132–3
spirituality 21–2
status, and power, within
    Christianity 132–4
Suffering Servant 136
Sullivan, John 165n

The Tamer Tamed
    (Fletcher) 76–7
The Taming of the Shrew
    (Shakespeare) 76
Tathyw of Caerwent 27
'This is how it happened'
    (*Fel hyn y bu*) (Waldo
    Williams) 145

Timothy, St, circumcision
    (Acts 15) 14
Titus 65
Tutu, Desmond,
    Archbishop 113, 123
two cities theory, Augustine
    of Hippo's teaching
    116

USA, and the doctrine of
    Providence 127
Usk river (Wales) 28

Venantius Fortunatus 150
Veniaminov, John (St
    Innokent) 95–8, 100
Vexilla Regis (David Jones)
    150–1, 152

Wales
  Celtic saints 27, 31, 32,
    35
  religious culture compared
    to that in America 6–7
Welsh Americans, religious
    culture compared to
    that in Wales 6–7
Welsh Church,
    disestablishment 36–7
Welsh language, Bible
    translated into 102–3
Welsh nationalism,
    suppression, compared
    to that of the Makah
    Indians 9

'We're still here' (*Ryn ni yma o hyd*) 8
Wesley, Charles 129
Whitby, Synod (664) 36
Wilfrid, St 36
Williams, Rowan, Archbishop 130–1
Williams, Waldo (poet) 55, 144–7, 149
Wink, Walter (American theologian) 116, 140, 141

woman with the issue of blood 79, 80–2
women
  in the Gospels 77–8
  place in African cultures 119–21
  social position affected by patriarchy 2–3
  subjugation 71, 75–6, 116–17

Yeats, W. B. 4